The Royal United Services Institu

CW01334645

War and Morality

Proceedings of a RUSI Conference: 'Morality in Asymmetric War and Intervention Operations' held on 19–20 September 2002

Including a new section on the Iraq War and its aftermath

Edited by Patrick Mileham

www.rusi.org

First Published 2004
© **The Royal United Services Institute for Defence and Security Studies**

All rights reserved. No part of this publication may be reproduced, stored in a retrieval system, or transmitted in any form or by any means, electronic, mechanical, photocopying, recording or otherwise, without prior permission of the Royal United Services Institute.

Whitehall Paper Series

ISBN 0-85516-186-8
ISSN 0268-1307

Series Editor: Dr Terence McNamee
Assistant Editor: Alanna Henderson

Whitehall Papers are available as part of a membership package, or individually at £8.00 plus p&p (£1.00 in the UK/£2.00 overseas). Orders should be sent to the Membership Administrator, RUSI Membership Office, South Park Road, Macclesfield, SK11 6SH, United Kingdom and cheques made payable to RUSI. Orders can also be made by quoting credit card details via email to: membership@rusi.org

For more details, visit our website: www.rusi.org

Printed in Great Britain by Stephen Austin & Sons Ltd. for the Royal United Services Institute, Whitehall, London, SW1A 2ET UK

RUSI is a Registered Charity (No. 210639)

Contents

Preface

Patrick Mileham

It is often very difficult to recall what was stated, thought or felt during a period of acute crisis. The heady days between 11 September 2001 and the actual invasion of Iraq was one such period. To make any sense of what happened, and any lessons to be drawn, we need to be reminded of prior expectations, particularly when placing a high moral value on the result of military actions. Some of the views expressed at this conference are obviously 'dated'. Most of what they say, however, endures.

The claim 'Force for Good', the government's justification for employing armed force, brings to centre stage the subject of 'military ethics'. We in Britain have found such a subject extremely difficult to address, preferring to remain vague. Is there a higher, moral course of military action, above that which the law specifically enables? This sort of question is now of much more urgent concern than hitherto, for every uniformed serviceman and woman in Britain, as well as politicians and statesmen. When is a war 'just' and what military means are justifiable? The public wants answers too.

The organizers of this conference are very grateful to the many speakers and contributors from Britain and abroad, who gave of their time, energy and expertise to make this conference such a memorable one. I personally am grateful to the Royal United Services Institute for staging this conference at a time that could not have been more appropriate. The debate will continue well into the future.

Foreword

Richard Cobbold

No day passes without more news from Iraq. The whereabouts, even the existence, of weapons of mass destruction are matters for interesting debate. The legal process appropriate for dealing with the toppled former President of Iraq is contentious, but at present hardly transparent. Burning questions persist about moral responsibility of politicians, service personnel, civil servants and the British public itself.

This conference, the third and largest in a series, took place in the week before Parliament first debated the prospects of war against Iraq in September 2002, and RUSI is but a quarter of a mile from the Palace of Westminster. We drew on the views of renowned international speakers and they provoked a vigorous debate amongst a distinguished audience. It was one of the better conferences RUSI has hosted in recent years.

The debate on the experiences of Afghanistan and Iraq will continue for many years. As well as being a faithful record of views on the 'morality of asymmetric war and intervention operations', I believe this Whitehall Paper will form a useful text for many groups of professional practitioners and observers, as well as military scholars. The close study of the 'Moral Component of Military Effectiveness' has become increasingly central to planning the future security and defence of Britain and other liberal democracies. Implementing an international policy of being a 'Force for Good' demands that every care is taken to ensure that this becomes a reality rather than just a label.

Rear Admiral Richard Cobbold is Director of RUSI.

Chapter 1

Global Violence

Global Violence

Mike O'Brien

Over the last decade we dealt with the aftermath of the Cold War. For the next ten years it looks like we will be dealing with problems associated with terrorism:

- Will terrorists be able to get access to Weapons of Mass Destruction and be willing to use them?
- Will more nations around the world currently suffering under bad governments collapse into failing states, giving rise to more terrorists?
- What should we do about it?

Woodrow Wilson tried to find a moral settlement to the aftermath of the First World War, with limited success. Today, we face a world where we cannot ignore failed or failing states. We know from experience that they will spread instability to their neighbours, and harbour terrorists that can strike anywhere in the world. Ignoring them is not an option.

But what are the rules that we should operate under? The two that are inextricably linked are international law and morality. The war against terror will test the morality of our position. Our society's response to asymmetric warfare and intervention operations will pose moral issues for all of us. Asymmetric warfare requires a response that can be military, political, economic or social. And there are moral implications to consider. Our response to terrorism may involve restrictions on our liberties. We must stop terrorists who may seek to use suicide bombing or chemical and biological weapons against us. In order to fight terrorists, the state may

---

Mike O'Brien MP is Minister of State, Foreign and Commonwealth Office and Minister of State for Trade and Investment in the Department for Trade and Industry. From 2002 to 2003 he was Parliamentary Under-Secretary of State at the Foreign and Commonwealth Office, where he was responsible for non-proliferation and security policy issues and counter-terrorism as well as a large part of the globe, including the former Soviet Union, Middle and Far East and Northern Africa.

need in particular circumstances to look at accessing certain emails, tapping telephones, carrying out tougher searches at airports, carrying out stricter security checks on those with access to sensitive installations, like nuclear reactors or water supplies and other services.

The paradox is that whilst the aim of fighting a war against terrorism is to preserve our freedom, in order to do that some of those freedoms may well need to be curtailed. Government will need to carefully balance the requirements of security against the importance of preserving the liberties we treasure. After all, the aim of terrorist action is to force the state to over-react, to take action that imperils its legitimacy.

Asymmetric warfare is not just about massive international intervention in a failed state, the strong against the weak. It can also be the weak against the strong, the terrorist attacking a strong society in the hope of using that strength against it to bring it down. This sort of asymmetric warfare aims to use the strength of the state against itself. Terrorists' power to inflict damage, notwithstanding 11 September, is limited. The state must of course react but it must do so in a proportionate way, recognizing that the aim of the opponent is to produce over-reaction. Under-reaction could be just as bad, however. It would be evidence of successful intimidation by the terrorist and of weakness. A balanced response is essential.

Asymmetric warfare can wreak its greatest damage by producing an ill-judged response by the state. That means that it is not sufficient for the state's response to asymmetric warfare simply to be for it to be effective in combating terrorism. In addition, it must be politically and morally tolerable to our culture and preserve our freedom. After all, when the Romans faced asymmetric warfare in their time they operated brutal repression – such as crucifixion – as a deterrent. Today, the BBC and CNN would likely make such disproportionate punishment politically impossible, as much as it would be morally reprehensible.

We cannot predict with sufficient accuracy all the potential asymmetric threats to our people, therefore we cannot protect everything against every risk. That means we have to think hard how we deal with law in society, about the threats that we are most likely to face and how we seek to protect ourselves against them. We will need to minimize the high-value targets for chemical and biological weapons, create a greater emphasis on special operations and counter-terrorism, and develop improved detection and identification systems for chemical and biological weapons.

Most importantly, we will need to improve our intelligence systems – both technical and human – for monitoring potential threats. We will need to mobilize our society to be aware of the threat, to have some understanding of how to deal with it, but we will have to be careful that in the process we do not frighten our people. Having dealt with an IRA threat for thirty years, the British people and their government are probably better able to respond in a proportionate way than almost any other country.

Asymmetric warfare can also lead us to intervene in a state which is failing or is a direct threat to us. The global coalition against terrorism demonstrates that when the moral case for action is clear, its force can be irresistible. There can be a moral case for intervention. As Kant said,

> There is an imperative that commands a certain conduct immediately, without having as its condition any purpose to be attained by it... this imperative may be called that of morality.

Afghanistan and Morality

In Afghanistan a year ago:

- a regime was in power which did not allow women to work (particularly serious in a country of up to 50,000 war widows), or girls over eight to attend school;
- over four million Afghans were living on the borders of neighbouring countries as refugees; and
- the country was in its twenty-second year of fighting since the Soviet invasion, with the front line just north of Kabul.

In Afghanistan now:

- there is an elected President, a multi-ethnic government and a political process for more representative elections in 2004;
- one and a quarter million children are now in school, and thirty per cent of them are girls;
- over one and a half million refugees are returning home;
- Kabul is being rebuilt, with the International Security Assistance Force (ISAF) warmly welcomed by Kabulis; and
- the nationwide war has given way to isolated security incidents.

These are important effects of international intervention in Afghanistan. But the object of the intervention was to avert the threat posed by Afghanistan being used as base for terrorist activities by Al-Qa'ida.

Here the results speak for themselves: we have broken the back of Al-Qa'ida activities in Afghanistan and the regime that supported them has been ousted. The situation is not ideal, but it is far better than before. Afghanistan has a chance of a new start.

Afghanistan was not a conflict of our seeking. I recall the debates in Parliament where people said we should not intervene in Afghanistan, that it would be another Vietnam, that it would set the Muslim world against us, that international law would not justify our taking action. But the decent people who were opposed to war were wrong.

In circumstances that have to be carefully delineated, military action is the right way to resolve a problem. Armed conflict is not always wrong, either morally or legally. It was right to enter the war against Nazi Germany in 1939. It was right to intervene in Sierra Leone, in Kuwait and in Kosovo. Likewise, it was a moral failure not to intervene over Rwanda and Srebrenica. The American General William Tecumseh Sherman said 'war is hell' – and I suppose he should have known!

So, can it be right to inflict war on other human beings? Since Aquinas and, indeed, before, the philosophers have said that the answer can be yes. In Afghanistan our responses had a clear moral justification. It involved a firm collective action following an unprovoked attack, demonstrating the degree of international solidarity against this outrage. We acted to prevent further attacks from the Al-Qa'ida base in Afghanistan. It was a proportionate response that did not target civilians and was aimed at a justifiable outcome, averting further imminent threats.

Failing States

Policymakers today face two central challenges in dealing with failed or failing states like Afghanistan under the Taliban. Firstly, to make the moral case for action earlier, even before our interests are threatened. Paradoxically, it is often easier to gain public and political support to deal with an acute crisis, than it is to act earlier to stave off the crisis in the first place. But experience suggests that the prevention of state failure rests on a scarce commodity: international political will. If we are to secure public and international support for action, we need to make the case for early engagement much more strongly.

Secondly, we have to make the moral case for action within the evolving legal framework. As Phillip Bobbitt argues in *The Shield of Achilles* (2002), for all its flaws and faults, the system of international law that has evolved since the Treaty of Westphalia in 1648 has ensured that more people have lived in greater peace and prosperity than would otherwise have been the case. In the latter part of the twentieth century, the UN has been at the forefront of international efforts to rescue states and set them on the path to recovery. Through its humanitarian aid programmes and peace-keeping troops, the UN has maintained global order and tackled state failure in many parts of the world, including the Balkans, Sierra Leone and Afghanistan.

It is not just about providing troops. The international community needs to address the underlying causes of a conflict: ethnic imbalances in government, disputes over natural resources, social inequality. This means we must be prepared to take on a long-haul job, when the newspaper headlines, and the political kudos, have all moved on elsewhere. In recent years, we have demonstrated such a commitment in Kosovo, in Sierra Leone and in East Timor. And as Afghan women would not be working now if we had listened to doubters about coalition action last autumn, so East Timor would not have celebrated its independence earlier this year without the vision shown by those seeking solutions to violence.

In all these cases, there is a clear moral good – the increased welfare and prosperity of ordinary people – that has come as a result of armed action. But some interventions are less easy to justify. Suez and Vietnam were examples where people have had serious doubts about the wisdom of intervention. How do we tell the difference?

International Law

Clear practical results like the ones I have described provide a useful but ultimately incomplete and subjective answer. Jeremy Bentham's 'greatest good of the greatest number' is a useful guide, but cannot be our only yardstick. The underlying principle has to be one of international law. John Foster Dulles once said, 'I confess to being one of those lawyers who do not regard international law as law at all'. His point was simple: not so much that international law did not exist, but how can it be law unless it is enforced?

Today, international law is a firm and impressive edifice. It does indeed rely on the consent of those who choose to follow it. But then, so does domestic law. It is indeed broken from time to time. But then, so is domestic law. It does need social and political pressure to encourage law-abiding behaviour. But then, so does domestic law. And when pressure is not enough, firm action is sometimes needed against law breakers in international law, just as it is in domestic law.

remember the words of Sir Thomas More in *A Man for All Seasons*. When Roper says that he would cut down every law in England to get after the devil, More replies:

> And when the last law was down, and the devil turned around on you, where would you hide, the laws all being flat? This country is planted thick with laws from coast to coast – man's laws, not God's – and if you cut them down... do you really think you could stand upright in the winds that would blow then?

This government recognizes that international law must be the basis of our security. It allows us to stand upright in a world in which some ill winds blow. Its strength rests on the determination of states to obey it. That is why we believe it is so important to deal firmly with Iraq's persistent flouting of international law by disregarding the UN resolutions in respect of its weapons of mass destruction. After 11 September, we must recognize that we face new threats and international law must develop and adapt to meet them. International law is constantly being developed. New situations require new responses and create new precedents.

Following 11 September, we faced an unprecedented situation. It was the threat of further terrorist attacks that was the legal basis for action in Afghanistan in self-defence. This is an example of the way international law has been applied in new circumstances. Britain plays a significant role in this process. As a permanent member of the Security Council, a leading member of NATO, and a committed supporter of international law, we are often breaking new ground.

When circumstances change, sometimes governments find themselves breaking new ground in international law, shaping its established principles to the needs of new problems. When we do this we are judged by the response of our peers and whether we are acting in a way that is based on a moral imperative. Returning to Kant, he argued that moral action is not just an action that you should do under particular circumstances, or a rule that applied to one person but not another, but rather one that everybody ought to do regardless of who, what, where, when and why. This was the basis for the first of Kant's 'categorical imperatives'– categorical because they were true in themselves, not based on any hypothetical conditions. He said: 'so act that the maxim of your will could always hold at the same time as a principle establishing universal law'. That is, act in a way that if a general rule was made based on your actions it would be a rule applicable to all countries at all times.

Saddam Hussein

To act morally and to measure that action by the response of other countries is important. If our peers accept that what we are doing is a proper, indeed a moral, response to the situation we face, it will become a building block for the development of international law. If the international community is eventually driven to intervene by Saddam's failure to observe his obligations under international law on WMD, some will doubtless question the morality of intervention.

We know about Saddam's ability to inflict misery on twenty million people, his own countrymen. As William Shawcross recently said so eloquently,

> He forced his way into power by murder and maintained himself there by murder...he has run a regime of terror at home and as far abroad as he was able. He has invaded his neighbours and used poison gas against Iraq's citizens.
>
> For years he has tried to manufacture and conceal outlawed weapons of mass destruction – chemical, nuclear and biological – and has sought to develop the missiles to deliver them, in defiance of international law and 16 United Nations resolutions.
>
> After his daughters' husbands defected to Jordan and revealed details of these programmes, he lured them back to Iraq and had them murdered.

How should we respond to Saddam's state's callous use of chemical weapons against his own people? How can we ignore Saddam's power-crazy determination to develop WMD and to threaten the region and the international community as a whole? Essentially, how should we deal with the threat posed by Saddam's immorality? We learnt the lesson of non-engagement by what happened in Afghanistan under the Taliban. It descended into war, despair, and became a haven for terrorists. We will not make that mistake again in Afghanistan. Nor should we make it elsewhere.

Saddam's fate is in his own hands. Military action is neither imminent nor inevitable.

But when and if the day comes for the international community to intervene in Iraq, our concern will, of course, be to act morally and legally, and to help the Iraqi people to the stable and secure future they so richly deserve after years of dictatorship.

To make the world a safer place means that military action must always be accompanied by a clear and attainable vision of a just outcome, which means working with the forces of reason and democracy in any particular country. Military intervention, despite the death and destruction it causes, is sometimes a moral thing to do. As politicians, we have to recognize that fact and take the tough decisions that follow from it.

Responses To Contemporary Threats

David Hobart

My purpose is to set the background to military threats and responses, showing the way that they have developed in recent years. There were already a number of themes and continuums before the events of 11 September 2001. It is the nature of the debate about those continuums and the relationship between them that are of particular interest.

Threats and responses – the pace of change

It has taken us ten to fifteen years to move from a position when British defence policy was couched in terms of 'role one, protection of the UK; role two, NATO alliance; role three, out of area'. This was the phraseology of the 1980s and the late 1980s in particular. In 1997 the Strategic Defence Review re-cast those roles, reordering them with regard to the UK, NATO, international organizations, our people and our interests, forming our first composite role. The second role has become that of being a 'force for good'. The relationship between the 'traditional defence role' on the one hand, and on the other the increasing efforts we put into being a force for good, requires us to strike a balance. The nature of the relationship of these two major roles goes to the heart of the debate and reveals where our efforts are likely to lead in the future.

So what was our immediate response to the events of 11 September 2001? The UK was very quick, in conjunction with the United States, to identify agreed campaign objectives. These campaign objectives were declared publicly in Parliament by the Prime Minister, at a stage when we had not even started the incremental defence review. To an extent, these

---

Air Vice-Marshal David Hobart is Assistant Chief of the Defence Staff (Policy) in the UK Ministry of Defence. An air engineer by background, he has served on the Directing Staff of the Royal College of Defence Studies and as Director of Defence Programmes.

new campaign objectives laid the ground for the new defence review. They provided guidance, yet because they were in the public domain, they were also in some sense constraining. We had to determine *how far* we could extend the examination of possible policy changes after 11 September 2001.

I would like to focus on two of them and the first one in particular, which was to 'eliminate terrorism as a force for change in international affairs'. Such an objective is very direct, but it introduces a concept of a 'threshold for terrorism'. If terrorism is not a force for change in international affairs, does it need eliminating? Does this make the world safe for terrorists who act below the threshold? Do we just focus on the threat of terrorism above that threshold? Is this a search for consensus, where everyone can agree what changes have occurred in international relations, but not everyone can agree on lower levels of terrorism and the definitional problems that abound? The answer is that we seem to have to accept the concept of threshold.

The second UK campaign objective – peace support – is fairly uncontroversial. Reintegrating Afghanistan into the world community is an excellent example of 'force for good'. It is nevertheless an extraordinarily short, succinct and, some would say, almost impossibly challenging objective. For example, the Donors' Conference in Tokyo voted US$10 billion for the reintegration of Afghanistan into the world community. The critics of that process might say that $10 billion is the life-cycle cost of a medium-sized American or European weapon system. $10 billion will go some way, but will go nowhere near solving the particular problem of reintegrating Afghanistan into the world community. It is worth repeating that Afghanistan's reintegration is almost impossibly ambitious as a military objective.

The UK's response was not just military of course, nor just diplomatic: it became effectively a whole series of parallel responses. Parallel responses were drawn up, for example, by departments within Whitehall, and they developed trans-national dimensions, in the sense that the activities of those departments tended to be external rather than internal. One obvious example is that of policing activities, designed to control domestic terrorism. Transnational activities with other nations' police forces would be a perfect example of Home Office engagement in this process. Another example would be the role of the national banks, which can turn on and turn off currency flows to terrorist bank accounts at a flick of a switch, simultaneously, all over the world. So parallel and transnational activities provide some solutions of controlling and destroying terrorism.

The new debate about defence roles took place in the Ministry of Defence and in the public domain in organizations, schools, universities and industry and also in other countries. We have identified six themes that seem to describe those continuums of threats and disputes.

Has anything fundamentally changed since 11 September? Depending upon where you ask the question in the world, you will get a different answer. Certainly from the UK perspective, at the time we thought the terrorists' concept of operations was something new; we thought the co-ordination and scale was something new. As military programmers and planners it may not be pleasant to admit that the events in New York and Washington were actually an impressive piece of planning. It is extraordinary how the routes and avenues used by the planners of 11 September managed to achieve something that completely bypassed and cut across all the traditional lines of communication in the Western world. The irony is that there is something for us to learn from the terrorists, rather than merely something to despise. And again 11 September certainly calls into question the role of geography as a useful framework for analysis. It cannot be ignored, but too much reliance placed upon geography has been shown to be largely mistaken. The most important matter really is not what our perspective was; the most important recognition was unarguably that the United States *did* perceive the events as a step change. Their subsequent approach emanates from that belief. Anybody who has been to Washington or New York since 11 September 2001 notices a feeling of 'being at war', but this is not something that is shared across the world. There is no global perception of being at war in the same sense as there is in the United States.

The second theme was that 'treating symptoms compounds the cause'. This was a real fear of ours as we were trying to put together answers, or some policy proposals, post-11 September. The tit-for-tat conflict that has been going on in the West Bank, Israel and Gaza over the last fifteen to twenty years persistently came into our minds. The extent to which Israel relies on high technology on the one hand, versus extremism in its many forms from the Palestinians on the other, together with the extent to which we are simply failing to address causes and compounding the problem by merely treating the symptoms, forced us to think, 'We must not repeat these mistakes', or perpetuate or compound the problems.

Coupled to this we then considered the problem of failed states. I think it is probably true to say that failed states are more likely to host terrorists than normal integrated and successful states. But terrorists do not have a monopoly to act in failed states. The poor governance of states prompts the sort of behaviour we are trying to eliminate. We have a number of friends worldwide who have autocratic governments: many are resource-rich, whose quality of governance we do not admire and diplomatically we seek to influence and enable change. That leads us to question the real motivation of terrorism. I am still not sure we have come close to understanding this problem. At one extreme, was 11 September the result of middle-class, middle-aged angst? Was it something more fundamental? What were the human dynamics that sparked off the anger that formed the background to the events of that day? I am not sure that simple cause and effect can explain this in traditional forms of analysis. There is a real possibility, and a worrying possibility, that there can be a level of evil that defies policy analysis and defies forms of prescriptive actions thereafter. It is a real concern, because all you can do is suppress, not solve, the problems, leaving the symptoms to be dealt with in the longer term.

The third theme is that of 'risks versus opportunities'. One can become very gloomy very quickly on the risks associated with fighting terrorism, so we consciously sought to divide the problem into that of risks and opportunities. I spoke of geography and the extent to which the further you are from the United States, the less there is a perception of an immediate threat and immediate risk. Different alliance partners have different views on the US response to terrorism. The closer one is to the US, both politically and culturally, the closer one tends to share their values. Prime Minister Blair's view was absolutely unequivocal and immediate; 'shoulder to shoulder' was his phrase describing the UK position *vis-à-vis* the US. The same cannot be said for a number of other European and western countries. There is an extent to which there is a desire to keep the Americans at arm's length, to avoid the supposed risk of association with the Superpower. This is connected with the matter I introduced earlier, the threshold for terrorism. If the concept of a threshold for terrorism is the only way that one can get multinational acceptance or consensus that a level of terrorism exists and it must be addressed by the whole of the civilized world, then that may be an acceptable price to pay. That includes deciding on levels of domestic terrorism of all types, including such as those connected with animal rights.

The fourth theme is that of unique, even ephemeral, events and circumstances in the sense that a one-off chance to act against terrorism has presented itself. If we do not crack terrorism this time, then the circumstances and the public mood may never come around again. That has further consequence of immediacy, in that it will enable, for example, widespread cultural and domestic political support for action against terrorism. There is a sense of 'seizing the moment', or it will not return.

The fifth theme is a peculiarly military one. Most military people have spent years basing their policy planning and prescription for action on threat planning. It has been directed toward the East for many decades – Germany in the 1930s and 1940s, Russia and the Warsaw Pact thereafter. The nature of planning against specific threats was something with which we became very familiar. Planning on 'vulnerabilities to society' is an altogether more difficult and more complex problem, beyond normal military means of resolution. At one extreme, an attack on a nuclear power station is something that we might not normally conceive as being a likely 'military target'. Making sure there is a domestic political response to the potential for attack on such a civilian target introduces a whole range of difficult issues. One ends up with the idea that 'risk management' is the only way to resolve this problem. An acceptable political response must include some combination of managing the many consequences aggregated together if the attack takes place. This marks a distinct change from the idea of threat planning to that of vulnerability planning. It is, however, extraordinarily difficult to come up with credible scenarios that relate to vulnerability planning. If we had tabled the events of 11 September 2001 as a scenario 24 hours earlier on 10 September, I suspect it would have been largely rubbished.

'Home versus away' is shorthand for the nature of the way that the UK has traditionally conducted its defence. For centuries we have sought to conduct our defence as far away from the UK's territory and waters as possible. A direct threat to the UK was therefore the result of the prior failure of this form of defence. The Battle of Britain in 1940 would be an example of something that was very, very close to our traditional historical approach breaking down. But certainly for the last fifty years the inner-German border has effectively been the line upon which UK national defence has been drawn. Now 11 September has started to change such thinking. The relevance of 'homeland security' as a defence concept has started to grow. Therefore we had to re-examine the balance between what we do to defend ourselves close to our own shores and territory, and what we can continue to do at arm's length. In some respects we will have to reaffirm that arm's length defence remains a valid concept.

In respect of homeland security, the claim that terrorism is a municipal crime, of prime concern to the Home Office, creates planning problems for the military. A certain series of contradictions follow. 'Terrorism by Air' is a matter on which the Ministry of Defence leads, while terrorism that comes by sea is not dealt with by the MoD. Inter-departmental disputes will come as no huge surprise. One further problem is of different capabilities of security and 'force design'. Clearly one needs a different range of capabilities for arm's length defence, compared with homeland defence. Also there is potentially a greater role for Reserve Forces in the context for homeland security than there is for defence overseas. In some respects this will prompt adjustments to the balance between Regular and Reserve Forces.

And the sixth and final theme is that it was felt to be very important that the UK approach to 11 September 2001 be a distinctive British-style contribution, consistent with the wider war on terror, as opposed to being merely part of a larger campaign by the Americans. Consequently we have sought to preserve a breadth of contributory actions in our response to 11 September. This is most easily illustrated by our performance in Afghanistan. On the one hand we provided the first commanders of the International Security Assistance Force (ISAF), seeking to stabilize the cause of the problems. On the other hand, elsewhere in Afghanistan, we were seeking to fight elements of the Taliban. And there is, from a planning and a cultural point of view, a further series of complications as you attempt simultaneously both to fight *and* to avoid fighting in the same country.

I would draw some conclusions from what I have asserted. I touched on balance of commitments. How much should we look to traditional defence, how much to 'force for good'? This leads very quickly onto the second question, 'how much force should we be prepared to use'? In today's world it is very, very difficult to design force structures. The traditional certainties, in terms of threat planning, have largely disappeared. It is now much more a question of what we want to do with our armed forces with a greater degree of discretion than we have achieved in the past, and the impact on world events we seek to achieve. That provides a less tangible basis upon which to shape the size of our armed forces and their capabilities.

The third conclusion is about the value of coalitions. One would say politically that they are absolutely essential. A whole series of organizational benefits accrue to being a member of a coalition. In purely military terms, the Americans may argue that coalitions have rather limited benefits, and it is often a series of minor enablers, such as host nation support and access to airfields and ports, that are important, rather than major, active contributions by nations in coalition. Extremes have to be reconciled and a balance reached.

Procurement of future weapons is a consequential problem too. Part of it is the nature of our targeting of those weapons and the extent to which we employ 'time-sensitive targeting', which is the way we fuse together intelligence and decision-making so we can use weapons rapidly. This causes a range of difficulties, not least that it is extraordinarily difficult to generate a guaranteed synthesis of all the factors. Time-sensitive and 'intelligent targeting' are the only ways of proper target discrimination in a military sense.

The last two points constitute a compounded problem we face in the future, namely public scrutiny and strategic surprise. The nature of public debate and media interest in military matters is ever more sensitive. The extent to which putative war plans are trailed in the press and on the television is, for many of us, the right and acceptable price to pay in a democracy. But I personally believe that there is a danger that immediate public scrutiny remains the single greatest inhibitor to a successful military campaign, with the minimum number of casualties. There is a real paradox there – perhaps paradox is the wrong word – there is a real dilemma. The appetite for public debate for such issues, which can be media-driven, rather than the press responding necessarily to public demand, does create real and lasting problems. Such constraints could produce a poorer military solution than one where we can achieve unfettered strategic surprise.

The response to 11 September 2001 is not the best example to describe the way we British go about our business. I came back recently from Sierra Leone, which is either at the top or bottom of virtually every league table that matters. Male life expectancy – it is at the bottom, at 39 years old. Income per capita – it is at the bottom, at $145 US dollars per head, per year. Infant mortality by the age of 5 – it is in the top 50 percent. In the last three years in Sierra Leone, British armed forces have contributed 17 500 personnel to UNAMSIL, the largest UN peacekeeping force that currently exists. We have been involved in a multinational evacuation operation; we have been involved in traditional peacekeeping; we have been involved in the new style of peace-support operations and we have been involved in active war fighting, albeit in small scale operations. That shows a combination of functions that, traditionally, you would never have expected could come together in a single country and in such a short period of time. All those functions have been carried out under the banner of 'force for good'. And I believe, in conclusion, that the British actually have a rather impressive story to tell. 'Force for good' is something at which we are getting better. It is a mission statement and good guide for our future defence policy.

Terrorism and Morality

Conor Gearty

Understanding the Language of Terrorism

Any analysis of the relationship between terrorism and morality must start with careful consideration of what is meant by 'terrorism'. Integrity in the use of language has moral value in its own right and, as we shall see, uncertainty in deployment of the concept of terrorism has exposed those who use it to allegations of hypocrisy and double standards. What the idea most obviously and uncontroversially connotes in its contemporary usage is the deliberate or reckless killing of civilians, or the doing of extensive damage to their property, with the intention of thereby communicating a political message of some sort to a third party, usually but not necessarily a government. Such violence is used as an alternative to more orthodox direct or political action, and is seen by those responsible for it as primarily a mode of expression. The protagonists of political terror are engaged in seeking to achieve some goal or other which is broadly political in the sense that it is separate from their own personal circumstances and/or their own private avarice.

It follows that the drunken father who beats up his wife to show who is boss within the home may be engaged in terrorizing a victim to communicate a message, but this is not political terror. Likewise, the bank robber who shoots a hostage in the vault to ensure that the rest of his captives stay silent is the purveyor of a different kind of terror. The deployer of terror for a political end is therefore, and it might be thought perversely, to be distinguished by his or her unselfishness; as one of the relevant legislative definitions in the United States puts it, the violence is designed to achieve something other than 'mere personal monetary gain'. These are not 'merely' capitalists with a peculiarly minimalist approach (even by the stan-

Professor Conor Gearty was Professor of Human Rights Law at King's College, London and is now Rausing Director of the Centre for the Study of Human Rights at the London School of Economics. He is a practising barrister in human rights law.

dard of capitalists) to the protective obligations of the state. We are dealing here with political actors, albeit (it might be thought) of a particular brutal (or as some might say, determined) sort.

I have little doubt in my own mind that sub-State actors whose only deployment of violence is of a terrorist kind fitting the core definition given above, are invariably involved in conduct that can rightly and confidently be described as immoral. Groups whose only engagement across the politico-military spectrum is the killing of civilians have nothing of any interest to say; if terrorism is, as Walter Laqueur so eloquently put it, 'the weapon of the weak', then I would add that terrorism of this sort is the weapon of the weak bully, lashing out at the defenceless so that all might see his (or her) pain. Subversive terrorism of this kind is also, I would say, always ineffective, for three reasons. First, with this kind of terrorism the medium becomes the message so completely that no one hears what else the terrorist claims he or she is trying to say. Who cares about all that oppression when we see the dead bodies of those decent non-combatants thrown from the aircraft or gunned down on the street or at the airport check-in? The brutality has gained the world's attention as it was intended to do, but the world then never sees past that brutality. Second, subversive attacks on civilians by terrorists who do nothing else are frequently counter-productive, viewed even in their own terms, because their effect is to provoke such massive state reaction that the groups themselves are destroyed. This was the experience of the South American 'urban guerrillas' of the 1960s and seems also to be the case with the perpetrators of the events of 11 September. Thirdly, such violence often destroys its own goals as well as those who deploy it, by making modest, peaceful agitation for the same ends almost impossible. Witness the difficulties the IRA campaign caused the SDLP in Northern Ireland before an essential constitutional solution was eventually achieved in the Good Friday Agreement, and observe also the problems generated at the present time by radical elements in Islamic societies for governments unsympathetic to fundamentalism. Each of these objections to subversive terrorism isolated from other kinds of military action is in my view sufficient to warrant the rejection of such violence; there can be few if any groups engaged in terrorist violence of this sort as their primary activity about which one or more of these points cannot be made.

It is important to note here that I am not judging terrorism to be morally wrong merely because I am calling it terrorism; rather, I am providing reasons why the conduct I have described as terrorism is also rightly to be viewed as perhaps immoral but certainly inefficacious: the label itself does not do this work alone. So far I have been talking entirely of subversive groups because this is the dominant discourse so far as terrorism is concerned. But if it is right to view 'political terror' in the way described above, as the intentional or reckless killing of civilians or damage to their property so as to communicate a political message, then it follows that 'terrorism' should be the noun that describes what those involved in 'political terror' do. A 'terrorist' is on this basis one who practices the technique of political terror, or 'terrorism'. Of course the 'terrorists' who carried out the 11 September attacks and who have been judged in such reprehensible terms were practitioners of political terror of this sort. But there are other purveyors of political terror around as well. Terrorism is a type of violence, not a type of person – a methodology not a group classification. It follows that it is a technique in international relations and/or domestic politics that is capable of being used by *any* player on the political or the international scene. It describes what people do, not what people are. Viewed from this perspective, terror as a tactic and terrorism as a description of that tactic is rightly to be seen as something that is available *both* to governments *and* to subversive groups. Political terror may be practised right across the political spectrum, from right to left, from the isolated revolutionary, through the guerrilla group and the secessionist to the forces of a state. In contrast to the 11 September terrorists, where political terror is practised by states and guerrilla movements it will be one method of attack among a variety available to be used.

Historically it has been states that have been most extreme in their deployment of political terror, the greatest in the sense of being the bloodiest exponents of terrorism. Clear examples from the past include not only the excesses of Stalin and Hitler but also the use of violence by central American governments in the 1980s and – perhaps most dramatically of all – the dropping of the two atomic bombs on Hiroshima and Nagasaki in 1945. The latter in particular was a pure act of political terror: 'look what we can do, now listen to us'. The same could be said of the United Kingdom's decision to attack German cities from the air during the latter part of the Second World War. Manifestly it is frequently political terror that the Israelis have been engaged in on the West Bank and Gaza Strip, just as it is what they often did in Lebanon in 1982 and on countless other occasions before and after. Civilians are attacked, deliberately or as a result of a reckless disregard for their safety, in order to say something to your adversaries that you judge cannot be communicated in any other way. I repeat that this is merely to describe these events, not to judge them; it is not impossible to envisage circumstances in which terror in a large and desperate conflict may not be by definition morally reprehensible, and it may be felt that some of the actions just described are justifiable on this basis. For present purposes that is neither here nor there: right or wrong, government terror is generally much more effective than subversive terror because states generally have better means of achieving their terror goals (e.g., tanks, airplanes, heavily armed troops and so on). A suicide bomber is also a terrorist on this analysis but all they have is themselves, a few bombs and a willingness to die: strengths certainly but nothing compared to being funded by the US Congress and equipped by the Pentagon (this may explain why contemporary governments engaged in political terror themselves are so anxious to talk up the mass destructive powers of their terrorist opponents; it is almost as though the asymmetry of the capacity for terror as between the two sides embarrasses them, and they want – if only in their propaganda – to level the playing field).

As indicated above, the notion of terrorism nowadays has a strong connotation of the subversive about it, and as a result it appears not easily to fit the kind of violence just described. The old dictionaries understood very well this simple idea of terrorism as a technique of violence available to all combatants engaged in war and war-like struggle. The 1951 *Concise Oxford Dictionary* described the 'terrorist' as

> One who favours or uses terror-inspiring methods of governing or of coercing government or community, esp. (1) Jacobin under reign of Terror, (2) Russian revolutionary.'

Indeed, it was from the Jacobins that we derived our modern phrase. But the language has moved on since the 1790s. Viewed from the contemporary perspective, several changes have occurred, all debilitating in their effect, and subversive of any attempt to achieve a coherent connection between terrorism and morality.

The first point to note is that the term 'terrorist' now describes a category of person rather than a technique of violence. The 'terrorist' is no longer (merely and relatively neutrally) the deployer of political terror, whether as government leader, guerrilla hero or ambitious revolutionary, and maybe as part of a wider military campaign, maybe not. The terrorist is always now a subversive, someone who opposes the established order either in his or her nation ('the domestic terrorist') or internationally (the 'international terrorist'). Secondly, the subversive today is landed with this 'terrorist' label even if he or she has never engaged in political terror as such, in the central sense of attacking civilians in order to communicate a political message. These latter day 'terrorists' may be merely challenging the power of the ruling elite, as are Mr Mugabe's 'terrorists' in Zimbabwe. Or they may be engaged in quasi-military operations against politico-military targets which are anything but indiscriminate. They may be no more than particularly robust eco-agitators or animal rights activists. Even if they are fighters engaged in a restrained military campaign against an undemocratic, racist or genocidally-inclined regime, in today's language they are still 'terrorists', with the government forces that oppose them being the 'counter-terrorists'.

Thirdly, in contrast to but following from these first two points, the forces of the established order are nowadays never themselves any longer categorized as terrorist. Instead, they are always now 'counter-terrorist', regardless of how violent they themselves are or how much more brutal and terror-inducing they are than those they oppose. This is because fourthly and finally, a moral judgement has insinuated itself into the language of terrorism. What the terrorist does is always wrong, what the 'counter-terrorist' has to do to defeat them is therefore invariably, necessarily right. The nature of the regime, the kind of action that is possible against it, the moral situation in which the violence occurs – none of these complicating elements matters a jot against the contemporary power of the terrorist label.

In its modern form, therefore, the language of terrorism has become the rhetorical servant of the established order, wherever it might be, and however heinous its own activities are. Talking of 'terrorism' in this way flattens the world of international relations, removing all the subtle peaks and valleys that make up the real life of nations, and reducing the diplomatic map to a dull, lifeless plain on which are arrayed the huge army of sovereign nations on one side (the 'counter-terrorists') and those who seek change – for whatever reason – on the other ('the terrorists'). It is obvious that this is a crassly ahistorical account of the world, ignoring how the various governments and regimes that deploy the language of terrorism in this way themselves secured power: there is a Cromwell, a Washington, a Mandela or a Mugabe behind most of today's political power structures. It is in the inconsistency of its approach to the use of force for political ends that the language of terrorism most exposes itself to moral disapprobation.

Evolution of the Modern 'Terrorist'

How did such a fantastic transformation in the meaning of the word come about? The answer is to be found in the Middle East, but the origins of the transformation begin elsewhere. The idea of the 'terrorist' as a type of person rather than a technique of violence grew out of the concept of the 'urban guerrilla' which in turn was a kind of revolutionary – mainly based in South America – who sought in the 1960s to bring Castro's and Che Guevara's insights about rural guerrilla subversion to the cities. Wandering around the forest looking for the state's army to attack was fine in certain circumstances but not a sure-fire recipe for revolutionary success in countries with large urban populations. The problem the 'urban guerrilla' soon encountered was that it was hard to attack the army in the city. It was usually well guarded and thus they went about the place cautiously. The police were easier to kill initially, but of course they also began to take precautions. So the 'urban guerrilla', in order to do something to justify his or her existence, had to expand the notion of the legitimate target: the retired police officer, the bank manager, the industrialist came within his or her sights, and carried with them the inevitable consequence of what we would call today 'collateral damage' – i.e. death or injury to persons who were not culpable, even on the urban guerrilla's broad estimation of moral blame.

In Europe, a few dilettantish groups sought to copy the urban guerrillas they had read about before they dropped out of university: in Italy the Red Brigades, in the United Kingdom the Angry Brigade, in Germany the Baader-Meinhof gang (afterwards the Red Army Faction). Even the United States had its Weathermen (then Weather Underground after complaints from feminist revolutionaries). Needless to say, these groups were not very popular. Western states and their citizens found their apparently indiscriminating violence to be as repugnant as it was mystifying. But at the time, between 1968 and 1972, the violence had quite an effect on the collective psyche of the West, provoking an anxiety out of all proportion to the harm actually done. More substantive in its effect was the secessionist violence that was also getting under way in the Basque areas of Spain, in the north of Ireland and (to a lesser extent) in Corsica and (across the Atlantic) Quebec. Here was more political terror, and a different kind of 'terrorism', one with broader support and a greater capacity to harm, but rooted – like the urban guerrillas – in a very wide sense of culpability and therefore of legitimate targeting.

Now consider where the Palestinian question and the PLO leader

Yasser Arafat fit in all of this. The first attempts to force Israel to allow a Palestinian state were entirely conventional, a model of how to conduct warfare on gentlemanly, Western-approved terms. The events of 1948 and 1967 are of course hotly disputed, but what is clear at least in 1967 is that various state armies from neighbouring Arab states attacked their Israeli neighbour, engaged with the enemy and sought to expel it from the region. No doubt there was some terror practised on both sides, just as there is in most warfare. The campaign was hugely counter-productive for the nations opposed to Israel, and lost Jordan and Egypt vast swathes of land to occupation. After the preferred option of straightforward war became unavailable, Arafat sought initially to establish a guerrilla operation in the occupied territories, to be the Michael Collins or Che Guevara of the region. Had it worked this too would probably have involved political terror from time to time, albeit as part of a wider campaign. The guerrilla initiative was, however, speedily ground down by the unrelenting nature of Israeli military might. It was only after these two failed manoeuvres that the Palestinian nationalists turned to isolated acts of political violence, as a kind of consolation prize only to be accepted because it was all that was available. It is in this sense that it is right to say that Arafat was a 'reluctant terrorist' and in this sense it is also absolutely right to describe terrorism as 'the weapon of the weak'.

This 'terrorism' by 'terrorists' also had little impact until – by an inexorable but dismal process of logic – it killed enough of the right people in the right places to command attention. This did not mean police officers in Israel or soldiers in the West Bank. It meant foreigners (especially Americans) anywhere and Israeli/Jewish people anywhere outside Israel. So we had hijacked aircraft, gun assaults in airports, and famously the attack at the Munich Olympics in 1972. Of course, the Israelis were responding in kind, attacking Palestinian areas, bombarding communities, shelling civilians, causing hugely disproportionate numbers of casualties; but they very cleverly managed to link the violence of their Palestinian opponents with that of the urban guerrillas and the quasi-colonial insurgents of the West under the general rubric of 'terrorism'. All this violence was all the same, 'terrorist' violence, which needed to be countered by the forces of civilization, which might in one place be the British bobby on the beat, in another the Israeli army in full battle cry. As Palestinian-related violence of this sort continued through the 1970s, conferences were held, academic treatises written, journals on terrorism studies quickly established. The future Israeli prime minister and 'terrorist expert' Benjamin

Netanyahu summed it up with the title to one of his many books on the subject, *Terrorism: How the West can Win*.

Even a cursory glance at the current situation in the Middle East quickly shows that there is indiscriminate terror against civilians on both sides, but especially (because they are better equipped for it) the Israeli side. Regarding subversive violence as the only kind of terrorism in the region leads inevitably to moral condemnation only of Palestinian actions. This trick with the truth is only possible because of the way in which the idea of the terrorist has come to be seen as a category of person rather than the purveyor of a type of conduct. We have stopped looking at what happens, and look instead at who is doing it. If the killer has a uniform on he or she is a 'counter-terrorist', a brave moral soul. If the victim has no army or government, then he or she must be an indiscriminate killer for political ends, a 'terrorist'.

Conclusion

The hegemonic potential of the language of terrorism, now given even greater force by the events of 11 September 2001, has ominous implications for domestic politics, both in Western states and further afield. The democratic breakthrough of the twentieth century was to make the secret vote of the people the *sine qua non* for the exercise of political power. But having the vote merely makes possible the struggle for a democratic culture, it does not guarantee such a culture. The imperatives of 'counter-terrorism' now matter more in places like Egypt, Pakistan and Saudi Arabia than any latent pressures to democratize that might otherwise have risen to the surface. Countries like Pakistan and Turkey rush to assist in the new American war, calculating correctly that their own 'counter-terrorist' actions will be strengthened and freed from scrutiny as a result. In the West, the events of 11 September have made possible a transformation in the atmosphere of democratic states, in the direction of an acceptance of an almost casual authoritarianism that would never before have been countenanced or permitted. The vote, already little used and cynically regarded, faces a challenge to its very rationale by the erection of a new and secret counter-terrorist super-structure, accountable to no one and with wide and uncertain powers.

Basic human rights, which prior to September 2001 were considered sacrosanct, have found themselves contested, and at risk of being mown down by the counter-terrorist juggernaut. There has been a frightening debate in the United States, in which members of the liberal elite have joined, about the appropriate use of torture – with safeguards and plenty of due process of course, perhaps even with a judicial warrant – but torture nonetheless. In Europe to our credit, and constrained in this instance by the European Court of Human Rights, we have refused both to torture our suspects or to pass them into the hands of our less scrupulous friends (as it is said the US authorities frequently do). But in the United Kingdom this has meant indefinite detention without trial for those whom we might otherwise have expelled; not torture certainly, but savage nevertheless when we remind ourselves that we are dealing here with people against whom sufficient admissible evidence cannot be found to bring criminal charges. (The United States produced no evidence to justify its demand for the extradition of a British-based man accused in a panoply of publicity last year of having trained the pilots who took part in the 11 September attacks. The man spent five months in custody in prison before being eventually granted bail. All charges against him were finally dropped when the one American minor offence he was accused of by the US authorities was reportedly exposed as never having occurred.)

The fight for human rights and democracy in the face of the challenges thrown up by this new age of counter-terrorism must involve traditional forms of popular protest and agitation. But it is also a struggle for integrity in the use of the language. The spuriously deployed notion of the 'terrorist' is the cornerstone of the counter-terrorist enterprise; if it can be dislodged, then it will be a small victory for many of the things that we hold valuable and which collectively help to civilize us: integrity in our use of language; honesty in our moral judgments; consistency in our approach to international affairs, and respect for the human rights of all and not just those we know. At very least, the political air would be easier to breathe if this vacuous fog of dangerous linguistic distortion could somehow be lifted. And further victories for human rights, civil liberties and democracy might follow.

Discussion

Weapons of Mass Destruction

It appears that the war declared against terrorism, following 11 September 2001, has been metamorphosed into the intention to remove weapons of mass destruction (WMD) from Iraq. The prominence and immediacy of the international debate, leading to UN resolutions on WMD, is inescapable. Their destruction in the months ahead is based on the clear imperative of radical change in the behaviour of the regime.

A regime change in Iraq has to be seen as a process, not an objective. The 'just outcome' following specific UN resolutions, and any subsequent actions taken by the international community to remove WMD, is to enable the Iraqi people ultimately to determine their own future. It has to be said that a build up of internal Iraqi 'pressure' seeking 'reason and democracy', is unlikely to set off an internal military process to replace Saddam Hussein. No decision has actually been made to date (19 September 2002) for external military intervention.

It has to be said that Saddam Hussein is a unique threat, and he has used WMD on his own people already. The containment by sanctions and weapons inspection was not working. For instance, inspectors were held for four days; guns were fired over their heads. Since their withdrawal in 1998 and the non-compliance of 16 UN Resolutions and 21 out of 23 Obligations, the current aim is to enforce Hussein's compliance within international law. The experience of 11 September 2001 taught the world that doing nothing about a threat of great magnitude can invoke double jeopardy.

There could be considerable internal chaos in that country, particularly if there is to be a war. There could, however, be a close parallel with what has been achieved in the stabilization of Afghanistan, imperfect thought it is, and any post-intervention situation in Iraq. In the event it seems sensible that Arab nations should provide stabilization forces, probably Egypt and Jordan.

Stabilizing a country after a military intervention, such as was the experience in Bosnia, Kosovo and Afghanistan, is a difficult and lengthy process. The war against terrorism and resolving internationally other specific threats could indeed take a very long time. While regrettable in retrospect, leaving countries like Afghanistan to suffer internal oppression for many years was partly to do with the constraints imposed by international law about intervention by external parties. More recently there has been a growing understanding and acknowledgment of a moral obligation to intervene in such nations' internal affairs. International law is developing.

Problems, however, do not come singly. All Arab nations continue to be very sensitive to the current situation in the Palestinian-Israeli conflict. There a solution can be sought concurrently with action against the more general Iraq threat. The programme of talks and actions, dealing amongst others with long-standing Security Council Resolutions 242 and 388, is likely to promote an improvement throughout 2003. If there is more than one grave threat to international peace and stability at any one time, we have come to realise that each must be dealt with, if necessary, simultaneously. It is best done by international coalitions and the consensus provided through the UN.

Terrorism

Manifestly the perpetration of an act of terrorism, which simultaneously can be a crime, or series of crimes, and a civil wrong, should be brought to the courts, using all charges under these categories that can be proved, to reinforce substantially the likelihood of terrorists' convictions. Despite the difficulties of proof, in such cases as that against Slobodan Milosevic, all 'crimes against humanity' must be brought before the courts, and one does not have to use the language of terrorism when bringing clearly criminal charges. Terrorism need not be made a crime itself, but is recognizable as a basis for suspicion of criminal conspiracy, enabling authorities to act within existing law and normal legal disciplines, so as to pre-empt and prevent such crimes.

While not inevitable, perhaps terrorism in future could be less often hosted by failed states, but more often provoked within failed cities, urban areas and townships. When control is lost by national institutions and governments, military engagement in urban areas imposes many additional ethical and moral constraints, in respect of military organization, equipment used and training.

There also continues to be a real dilemma and growing tension between maintaining strategic surprise on the one hand and on the other, the increasing ability, provided by the media for the public to scrutinize operations by security forces. The public are able to judge the morality of what the military do and the asymmetry of force used. This was noticed particularly during operations in Mazar-i-Sharif in Afghanistan by special Forces and in America after 11 September 2001, the question being what should and should not be published and broadcast by the media in attempting to interpret the truth, yet not compromise the immediate security of the operations. The speed of military operations and the immediacy of public reporting should not be a race.

Language

One has to take care with words and the meaning of words. The word 'innocent' is entirely normative to most of the world's peoples, but not to some terrorist groups who identify all their victims as guilty. Often their logic is to pick soft targets when so-called 'legitimate' military targets are too well defended. Similarly, any expansion of the definition of 'culpability' by terrorists must be deemed completely implausible, even evil. Terrorists have carried out wanton and 'reckless' acts against target populations, as witnessed in Northern Ireland, South America and in Al-Qa'ida activities.

We also have to learn precisely to define terrorism and interpret correctly terrorists' intentions. In destroying a building such as the World Trade Center, they are stimulating a fearful image of all buildings being attacked, in the imagination of the target public. This differs from quasi-military groups' and guerrillas' tactics: their targets are chosen for specific military advantage. The 11 September 2001 attack on the Pentagon was thus more a military act than pure terrorism. In any event, pictures and images have far more imaginative impact than words, transcending borders and languages so that everyone worldwide knows what has happened. The moral significance of these distinctions is to define acts by immediate purpose and longer-term intent.

Furthermore, large-scale terrorist violence may have obsessive religious and ideological dimensions, recalling the language of the 'infidel' and the 'crusade', contradicting the supposed universality of human rights. Such tendency to use violence has to be overcome as a long-term process, by education and positive international dialogue between people of all faiths and cultures. There needs to be a new international idealism of universally held norms and concepts, as well as practices. Indeed there is the growing possibility of a truly consensual United Nations, with the potential and capacity not only to act, but to effectively enforce Security Council Resolutions.

Moral Argument

Other awkward factors can be found amongst the moral arguments which seem fully to justify the need to use of force in specific circumstances, for instance to weaken the civil population's willingness physically to resist, or more generally affect their morale. The Germans 'justified' their bombing of Guernica (in the Spanish Civil War, 1937) and the US justified the use of atomic bombs on Japan in 1945. How close these acts were to charges of dishonour, immorality or even terrorism, cannot be ignored, although the disciplines of normal legal processes and law itself can be useful. This is particularly so when dealing with the imposition of constraints on human rights. Accidental injury to, or manslaughter of, civilian non-combatants remains undoubted fact. The accusation of double standards is inevitable and frequent.

The fact that failed states apparently export individuals and groups, intent on bringing their grievances to the attention of host countries by terrorist acts, is another moral conundrum that cannot be ignored. The terrorist events of 2001 were planned as much in London, Rome, Hamburg and Madrid, as in the US itself. This is a policing and intelligence gathering problem, more than it is directly military. There is a need, firstly, for much greater 'hearts and minds' understanding, to isolate criminals from law-abiding immigrants within ethically diverse societies. Then, there must be much political and diplomatic pro-activity, to prevent deepening antagonism between otherwise well-meaning nations, intuitively and unjustly suspected of complicity or sympathy with evil acts, for example, because they happen to be Muslim co-religionists.

Finally, the question of the secularization of human values cannot be ignored, if there appears to be a deterioration of security at the same time. 'Secular' human rights cause additional tension with some religions, yet unalloyed evil can hardly be described in any other words. Secular societies, seeking to preserve the rights and lives even of ill-disposed individuals, may thereby weaken the freedoms and even the security of the greatest number. International law draws on the Judeo-Christian tradition and chivalry for instance, making assumptions about the protection of women from injury and death in, and as a result of, combat. Other religious traditions see such matters differently. Morality can be defined with both the objectivity of law and the subjectivity of beliefs, which values the individual equally – victim, soldier or terrorist. Some of the pressure and lobby groups, so necessary to the moral debate and most concerned with monitoring what happens, are religiously motivated, and rightly so.

Chapter 2

The Just Use of Force

Legal Justification for the Resort to Force

Christopher Greenwood

One of the most important points I want to make about the legal justification for military action is that it matters – and not just to the lawyers, it matters to the military. International law is only partly based on the construct of academics, barristers, solicitors and other people sitting in ivory towers. It is not just the preserve of those of us who sit and argue in court after the event. It is a subject that has been created and built up over the years by the practitioner. And the practitioners for these purposes are the military, the diplomats, the politicians: people of far more significance than the lawyers and academics.

First of all it is necessary to give a brief outline of the legal regime relating to the justification for resort to force. Then it is necessary to look perhaps in a little more detail at the two case studies that are problematic for everyone today: namely the use of force in Afghanistan in the aftermath of 11 September last year; and the possibility of the use of force against Iraq over the course of the next few months. I am going to focus, therefore, entirely on the use of force at the international level. I am not going to enter into questions about the use of force within a state, such as the situation that has appertained in Northern Ireland. I only need to say in passing that the legal regime there is arguably even more important than it is in relations between states, and that had we invested ten per cent of the effort we currently invest in human rights activities in Northern Ireland in the early part of this century, in the 1960s, 1950s, 1940s, or even 1840s, I very much doubt we would have the problems we have had there in the last thirty years.

To begin with the most important current feature of international

Professor Christopher Greenwood has been Professor of International Law at the London School of Economics since 1969 and is a fellow of Magdalene College, Cambridge. He is joint editor of *International Law reports*, and is a leading international law barrister.

law, perhaps the biggest single change from the legal regime that existed at the time of the First and Second World Wars, is that you start today from the position that a general prohibition exists on the use of force in international relations. Codified in Article Two, Paragraph Four of the United Nations Charter, it is much more than just a written piece of treaty law. It is the fundamental principle around which the international legal system is expected to revolve, specifically that it is unlawful for one state to threaten to use force, or to resort to the use of force, against another. Now that general prohibition is of course subject to important exceptions, which I shall cover later. But it is absolutely vital to realise that when we talk, for example, about the use of force in the 'national interest' it may very well be that there are excellent political reasons for not resorting to force, unless it is in the interest of the state concerned. But the fact that the use of force may be perceived to be in the interest of a state is no longer a legal reason for resorting to it. Force is not simply an instrument of policy; it is something to be used, if at all, within the framework of the law. Therefore none of the legal justifications for military action which you would have found as commonplace only a comparatively short time ago – 'America's manifest destiny to occupy an entire continent'; 'interests of the British Empire'; 'vital strategic necessity' – today justifies resorting to military action.

Now, the devil is always in the detail in this area of the law, so what are the exceptions? In the form of words in which it appears today in the UN Charter, the right of self-defence, individual or collective, is justified if an armed attack occurs against a state. Now we need to look a little more carefully at what that means, because whereas every international lawyer agrees that there is such a right and that it is a fundamental part of the legal system, it is very hard to put two of us together and find that we agree on every feature of what the right of self-defence actually entails. This may be simply a reflection of the fact that it is difficult to get two lawyers to agree on any subject. In many respects it is our duty to find areas of disagreement.

The first point is that critical phrase 'if an armed attack occurs'. Do you have to wait for the shooting to start? In the words of a strategic doctrine that was much bandied about twenty or thirty years ago, need you sustain an initial casualty? That is not a new argument; it is certainly not something that has emerged since the Administration in the United States started talking about 'pre-emption', or since the 11 September 2001. It is an argument that goes back well over 150 years. A controversial question indeed, but it seems to me that there is very clear state practice – and states do make rules of international law – that they *believe* they are acting in accordance with the law, rather than what academic critics like myself might say.

There is very clear state practice in support of the proposition that, first of all, there is *no* right of 'pre-emptive self-defence', if what is meant by pre-emption is that you take military action today to address a threat that might materialize at some unspecified stage in the future. Secondly there *is* a right of self-defence against an imminent armed attack. 'Anticipatory self-defence' is what lawyers call it. Now the problem, of course, is that we do not all use the same language. What George W. Bush meant when he talked about pre-emption may very well turn out to be what I mean when I talk about anticipatory self-defence.

But there is a very clear dividing line between the two and it is illustrated by a case of some years ago when Israel attacked Iraq's nuclear reactor outside Baghdad in the early 1980s. State after state in the Security Council debate on that subject took the position that, while there can be a right of anticipatory self-defence against an imminent armed attack, this did not fit the case. It was not an example of an imminent threat facing Israel. Now one can argue endlessly about whether that was the right assessment of the facts of that particular case, but it does give some support for the proposition that anticipatory self-defence is part of international law, while a broad adoption of pre-emption is not. I shall turn shortly to what we might mean by an imminent threat for these purposes.

A second feature of self-defence is that it is not just the defence of one's own state; it can be the defence of other states as well. The United Kingdom would have been perfectly entitled to use force against Iraq in 1991 justified as collective self-defence in connection with Kuwait. No-one doubts that Kuwait had been the victim of an armed attack. Kuwait had requested British military assistance in a splendidly drafted letter, which echoed virtually every rule of international law imaginable. It appears that either the Kuwaiti government had taken with it into exile all its law books, or possibly there had been a certain amount of assistance from London or Washington in the drafting of this letter.

The third point to note is that the right of self-defence is subject to a right of pre-emption by the United Nations. The right of self-defence exists in international law, as it does in domestic law, only until global authority reasserts itself: until the Security Council has taken the measures necessary to restore international peace and security. That constitutes strong justification for military action in today's world.

The second justification would be action under a mandate from the United Nations. This is something none of us would have worried about until twelve years ago, but it now very much a feature of international life. Under Article 39 of the UN Charter, the Security Council has the authority to identify that a particular situation is a threat to the peace, an actual breach of the peace, or an act of aggression. The third reason is one that it has never actually used. Once the Security Council has made that determination, it can either take military action itself (if it had armed forces, which it does not) or, which is more practical, it can authorise military action by others. That of course is precisely what happened in the case of Kuwait, when Resolution 678, adopted by the Security Council in November 1990, authorised states to co-operate with the government of Kuwait to use all necessary means to achieve certain objectives listed in the resolution.

The next possible justification, much more controversial than the others, is a right of humanitarian intervention. The threat of an imminent humanitarian catastrophe within a state, or indeed the actual existence of such a catastrophe, requires or impels other states, either acting on their own or acting under a UN mandate, to intervene and put a stop to the situation.

Today there is broad agreement that you can act if the Security Council authorises it, which places the justification in the second of my categories rather than the third. But I would go further and say that in a situation such as existed in Kosovo there is a right of unilateral humanitarian intervention, even without a Security Council mandate. I would, however, have to acknowledge that that is far more contentious than either the right of self-defence or the mandate from the UN. Nothing else, in my opinion, would justify the resort to military action under modern international law – no right of pro-democratic intervention; no 'Brezhnev Doctrine' to stop the backsliding of a state from socialism; no 'manifest destiny'. The case for military action must be brought within one of the three exceptions to the general prohibition.

Moreover, this raises the question of whether it is lawful to use force at all. The fact that one has a just cause for resorting to force does not in any way detract from that other rule of law, which is that the way in which force is conducted must itself comply with the laws of war and, in certain circumstances, with human rights law as well.

With these preliminary remarks in mind, let me turn to the Afghan and Iraqi cases and try to provoke some discussion about both. Now in the first of those two, in the aftermath of the attacks of 11 September last year, the immediate problem for the lawyer is how to characterize the situation. Is the response counter-terrorism or war? Was the attack on the World Trade Center a grotesque crime under international law, or was it a first shot, or most recent shot, in a war between two parties? What I would like to suggest to you is that it is not a simple question of 'either/or'.

There are situations in which both of these questions can be involved. There is no doubt at all that the attack on the World Trade Center, in particular, the hijacking of the four aircraft and the attack on the Pentagon also, were crimes under international law. I could give you a long list of crimes not just under United States domestic law, but also under various international treaties. There is no doubt whatever that the United States' courts would have jurisdiction over those involved in planning this operation who are still alive today. There is no doubt either that international law courts in other countries could exercise jurisdiction over these crimes. But the fact that it is a criminal offence does not mean that it cannot also reach a level of gravity that involves the law on the use of force as well. Surprisingly, there was a fair degree of controversy about this amongst the academic international legal community, but I do not think there was any controversy amongst the practitioners at all. The Security Council Resolution 1368 (adopted unanimously on 12 September 2001), Resolution 1373 (adopted a fortnight later), the decision of the North Atlantic Council on behalf of NATO states and the decision of the Council of the Organisation of American States all referred to what happened as an 'armed attack' on the United States. In my view there is no reason whatever why an armed attack must emanate from another state rather than a non-state actor. The case that is always taken as the *locus classicus* of the law of self-defence is the incident known as *The Caroline* case between Britain and America in 1837. Groups of state-supported terrorists (as we would now call them) operated out of United States waters, attacking targets in southern Canada. *The Caroline*, the ship from which they were operating, was attacked in American waters by a group of British soldiers. It was destroyed, and one person was killed. Throughout the discussion of *The Caroline* case it was taken for granted that the concept of an armed attack could emanate not just from a state, but from a group of private individuals. There is no doubt whatever that the gravity of what happened on 11 September meets every possible criterion of intensity or international significance.

The difficulty, therefore, is not whether this was an armed attack, which might justify American military action by way of self-defence, but whether the action that was actually taken against targets in Afghanistan can fit within that regime of self-defence. In my opinion it can. It is much easier today to justify that action than it was back in October 2001, because we now know much more about the relationship between the Taliban regime and the Al-Qa'ida organisation. And I think you can make a very good case for saying the Taliban, the *de facto* government of Afghanistan at the time, was itself a party to the attacks on 11 September. Its relationship with Al-Qa'ida was close. But even if you could not, I still believe it would be possible to justify as self-defence attacking a terrorist organization, which is itself carrying out attacks of the kind we saw last year and which is being given free rein to operate from the territory of a state. It is not the case that the Taliban government could not have stopped Al-Qa'ida. The fact is that it did not do so. Nor is it the case that force was resorted to before any other option had been tried. If you look at the Security Council resolutions on the Afghan question before 11 September last year, they are very explicit about the obligations of Afghanistan not to allow its territory to be used in this way and to surrender for trial Osama bin Laden and various other named individuals.

However, there are two further problems. The first is that self-defence is dealing with a problem of now, not a problem of yesterday. The fact that you were attacked in September is not itself a justification for a military response in October. If you cannot respond to an armed attack while it is taking place, a later military response can only be justified by reference to the principle of anticipatory self-defence. It is a response not to what has happened but rather to what you expect, on the basis of last month's events, is going to happen next day, next week, next month.

Now there again I think you can make a good case for saying that the United States was quite right in taking the view that, having attacked New York and Washington in September last year, Al-Qa'ida was not going to stop at that. But was it an imminent threat? The difficulty here, I think, is that in assessing what is an imminent threat, you have got to take account of two factors, which would not have been an issue at the time of *The Caroline* dispute in the 1830s. The first is the gravity of the threat. When you are taking about whether a threat is imminent, it surely makes a difference whether you are considering the possibility of a car bomb with some Semtex in it, or a nuclear weapon going off. The scale of the danger must be a factor here and it is interesting that, in an opinion that was otherwise very critical of the British government's position, Rabinda Singh, a leading human rights lawyer, took precisely this point in his article in the *Times* (17 September 2002).

The second factor is the manner of the delivery of a threat. An imminent threat from regular armed forces, particularly something like an armoured incursion, is a great deal easier to pinpoint in time than a threat posed by a terrorist movement that relies on the hijacking of civilian aircraft, carried out by cells which are extremely difficult to penetrate and which can operate on a more or less global basis. So, when one asks whether a threat is imminent, I think it makes a big difference whether you are talking about Iraqi tanks moving up to the border of Kuwait, or the possibility of a lightning strike of some kind for which no immediate warning is evident.

The next problem area is that any military response has to meet the requirements of proportionally and necessity. You should not use force unless it is necessary to do so. That maxim, to which General Irwin refers [*in chapter* 4] about counter-terrorist activity in Northern Ireland, is every bit as potent when you are looking at international law relating to self-defence. In addition, the response must be proportionate. Now that, unfortunately, is a term that has a rather bad pedigree. When we talk about proportionality, first of all you only have to mention it to people in the American military and their mind goes back to restricted rules of engagement, as they considered them at the time in Vietnam, and they have a panic reaction. The press tends to assume that it is a matter of weighing up the number of casualties in the World Trade Center with the number killed in Kabul. If you compare the two sets of figures, as soon as you have more dead in Kabul than you had in the World Trade Center, the test of proportionality seems to be fact. However, it is not a matter of simple arithmetic at all. Proportionality is not a backward-looking matter, it is rather what is necessary to guard against a particular threat, without destroying what in the end you are seeking to protect.

The case of Iraq is far more controversial. The background will be well known, but let me just mention one feature of it. In November 1990 the Security Council gave an authority in Resolution 678, not to all states, but to those states cooperating with the government of Kuwait, (a formula which of course neatly excluded Israel), to use 'all necessary means' to deal with the invasion. It was a phrase that everyone has now picked up. I should warn you that Security Council resolutions are not drafted with exactly translucent clarity. They make a British Act of Parliament look positively 'user friendly'. In fact one colleague of mine in the Foreign Office legal department used to refer to a treaty as a 'disagreement reduced to writing'. A Security Council resolution is an even better example of a disagreement reduced to writing. One can always find a form of words that means different things to different people: in a sense, that is the diplomat's art. Unfortunately it is the lawyer's problem after the event. At the time, what was stated was that magic phrase 'all necessary means', which we all knew meant military action and could not have meant anything else in 1990. The purpose, everyone assumed, was to liberate Kuwait; but that is not what the Resolution says. It said that all necessary means were to be used to ensure that Iraq withdrew from Kuwait and complied with the existing Security Council resolutions and to restore peace and security to the region. The last point is critical, because one must take another step to Resolution 687 (adopted at the end of the war) that laid down the criteria Iraq had to accept to bring the hostilities to an end. It is known amongst diplomats and lawyers as the 'mother of all resolutions', the longest resolution at the time.

Resolution 687 is widely perceived as the basis of an agreement between Iraq and the Security Council because the Iraqis had to accept it formally. It is not an agreement at all. It is not the equivalent of a peace treaty, or even a cease-fire agreement. It is binding on every state in the world, because it is a binding decision of the Security Council. Iraqi agreement is not necessary to make it binding. The first paragraph reaffirms all the earlier Resolutions on the Iraq/Kuwait situation and then goes on to maintain them in force, except as expressly changed by the subsequent provisions of the Resolution. Amongst those provisions is a requirement, in paragraph 8, that Iraq remove all weapons of mass destruction – nuclear, biological and chemical – as well as the capability to manufacture those weapons, and all missiles with a range of more than 150 km.

It is now perfectly apparent that Iraq has not complied with that part of Resolution 687. The question, therefore, is whether or not there is a legal basis for the use of force against Iraq today. And there are I think three bases in which you could justify military action, subject very much to the exact facts of the case. The first is an easy one. The Security Council could find that Iraq is still a threat to international peace and security and issue a fresh authorisation for military action. If that happened then I think the legal basis for military action is put beyond any doubt. The second possibility is that you consider all the existing Security Council resolutions relevant to the case. That is no easy task; there are more than twenty of them. But in my opinion, there is a better case to be made here than has been made so far in public discussion.

There has been no express revocation of Resolution 678 in Resolution 687. The authority to use military force is still in existence: the question is only what triggers its application in a particular set of facts. And here I think the fact that Iraq remains in violation, and that that violation poses a threat to international peace and security, would be sufficient to revive the authority, or rather to maintain and allow reliance on the authority in Resolution 678. But there are two critical questions to answer. Is Iraq in breach, and what is the evidence? And secondly, much more telling, what is the evidence that Iraq's breach is a threat to international peace and security? Breaches of other kinds may be very important, but not as critical as this question. Iraq is also clearly in violation of its obligation to cooperate on the missing persons' issue. Its behaviour has been scandalous and no one has taken any notice: but that failure does not raise a potent threat to peace and security.

The third possibility would the right of self-defence and here, I think, you would have to show much the same material as is necessary in respect to the Security Council mandate. It is not enough, in my opinion, to show that Iraq has, or may, acquire the capacity to manufacture a nuclear weapon. The International Institute for Strategic Studies Report shows pretty potent evidence that Iraq is in a position to acquire that capacity in a fairly short timescale. You have got to go further, as Michael Quinlan said in a radio interview at the beginning of the summer of 2002. You have got to show, not merely capacity, but intention to use such weapons.

I have no ready answer to the question of 'intent'. All I can do, as a lawyer, is to try and set out the framework. What I have tried to do is firstly to suggest the questions you need to ask and secondly to indicate the evidence you need to look for, if military action against Iraq is to be justified.

Terrorism and International Humanitarian Law

François Bugnion

The terrorist attacks of 11 September 2001 against New York and Washington and the ensuing conflict in Afghanistan suddenly brought international humanitarian law into the limelight, but these tragic events have also raised fundamental questions about the relevance of international humanitarian law to the challenges posed by international terrorism.

Does international humanitarian law apply to what was immediately labelled as 'the global war against terror'? Does it adequately meet the need for humanitarian aid provoked by new conflicts? Some voices in the United States and elsewhere have questioned the relevance of humanitarian rules to the environment created by this new form of war. Humanitarian law has been declared outdated, out of touch with the new situation, or even an obstacle to the fight again terror.

As you know, the law of armed conflict developed out of the confrontation on the field of battle between sovereigns enjoying equal rights. Similarly, the first treaties regulating warfare and protecting victims of war – the Geneva Convention for the amelioration of the condition of the wounded in armies in the field of 22 August 1864, the St. Petersburg declaration on explosive bullets of 1868 and the Hague Conventions on land warfare of 1899 and 1907 – applied between the parties to those treaties, namely between states.

However, international humanitarian law also found a way to protect the victims of non-international armed conflicts, initially through the classic mechanism of recognition of belligerency, mainly developed in British and American doctrine and practice, and then through the adoption of specific treaty provisions: both Article 3, common to all four Geneva

---

Dr François Bugnion is Director of International Law at the International Committee of the Red Cross, which he joined in 1970. He has worked in Israel and the Occupied Territories, Bangladesh, Turkey, Cyprus, Chad, Vietnam and Cambodia and acted as Delegate General for Eastern Europe and Central Asia.

Conventions of 12 August 1949 and Protocol II of 8 June 1977 additional to those Conventions protect the victims of non-international armed conflicts, in other words civil wars. Because of the fundamental nature of the obligations they enshrine, these provisions are binding on any government confronted with a civil war and on the adversarial party as well.

The question therefore arises: does international humanitarian law apply to 'the war against terror', whatever this concept may cover?

First of all, I would like to point out that humanitarian law is based on the fundamental principle that the civilian population must enjoy immunity against the effects of hostilities and on the obligation to distinguish at all times between combatants and civilians and between military objectives and civilian safeguards. In order to avoid endangering the civilian population, combatants are required to distinguish themselves from civilians while carrying out military operations.

Since terrorists usually direct their attacks against civilians, so as to spread maximum terror, and fail to distinguish themselves from the civilian population, so that it is impossible to identify where the threat comes from, terrorism clashes with international humanitarian law at a fundamental level. Indeed, terrorism – whatever form it may take – may be considered as the utmost affront to humanitarian principles and rules. The two Protocols additional to the Geneva Conventions expressly prohibit 'acts or threats of violence the primary purpose of which is to spread terror within the civilian population'. Humanitarian law therefore unequivocally and unreservedly condemns any form of terrorism, from whatever quarter it may come, whatever its objectives and whatever cause the perpetrators claim to serve.

But still the question arises: does international humanitarian law apply to 'the war against terror'?

Actually, 'the war against terror' covers different types of action: police action, prosecution and trials, diplomatic action, financial initiatives to freeze or seize assets related to terrorism, etc. *Prima facie*, international humanitarian law does not apply to such activities; these are regulated by other branches of law. Nor does humanitarian law determine what is legitimate use of armed force, or the right to self-defence or response to aggression. These issues are regulated by the United Nations Charter.

On the other hand, whenever States resort to military force to fight terrorism – as was the case in Afghanistan as of 7 October 2001 – there is no doubt that such operations are covered by international humanitarian law. The decisive factor here is not the nature of the initial aggression but the response to it. This is the position which the International Committee of the Red Cross set out in a memorandum sent to the United States, the United Kingdom and Afghanistan on 5 October 2001, shortly before the opening of active hostilities, to remind them of the humanitarian principles and rules applicable in the impending conflict. No challenge was made to the ICRC position. On the contrary, the White House confirmed in a statement on 7 February 2002 that the Geneva Conventions did indeed apply to the armed conflict in Afghanistan, even though serious differences of opinion emerged concerning the legal status of combatants captured in Afghanistan and transferred to Guantanamo Bay.

Does applying the Conventions mean that persons protected by international humanitarian law are immune from legal action and prosecution? Certainly not. Prisoners of war and civilians protected by the Fourth Geneva Convention can be prosecuted for crimes committed, either during captivity, or prior to their capture. If grave breaches of the Geneva Conventions have been committed, the detaining power is not only authorized to prosecute the suspects under its jurisdiction, it is actually obliged to do so.

The criticism has been levelled that implementing the Geneva Conventions would afford suspects judicial guarantees of such magnitude that it would be impossible for the courts to convict the guilty, or that the accused would enjoy almost unlimited possibilities of appeal.

What the Third Geneva Convention stipulates, in fact, is that 'prisoners of war can be validly sentenced only if the sentence has been pronounced by the same courts and according to the same procedure as in the case of members of the armed forces of the detaining power'. In other words, international humanitarian law is referring to domestic law – it requires the States to respect the same standards that they have set for members of their own armed forces.

It has also been alleged that humanitarian law does not apply between a State and a non-State actor with international connections, such as the Al-Qa'ida network.

It is obvious that the 1949 diplomatic conference that drafted the Geneva Conventions now in force, basically had two situations in mind: either an international armed conflict between two states or coalitions of states, or a non-international armed conflict taking place within the borders of a single State. But what we are now witnessing is a confrontation between a coalition of states, led by the United States, and a non-state entity active in a number of countries. In this respect, a new situation does indeed exist, a situation that the drafters of the 1949 Conventions, as far as I know, did not foresee.

However, there is no territory that is not under the sovereign authority of some state. Apart from the high seas, there is no *res nullius*. Therefore, the following situations may arise. Either a government protects a terrorist network on its territory, as did the Taliban regime in Afghanistan, and foreign intervention to eradicate that network results in an international armed conflict, or the government concerned tries to neutralize the terrorist groups active on its territory, as is presently the case in the Philippines. This results in a non-international armed conflict, at least as long as external intervention in support of the government is not so massive that it fundamentally alters the nature of the conflict.

Underlying the legal arguments just mentioned, is the feeling that it is abhorrent to claim that the same set of rules should apply to those who conceived and planned the 11 September aggression (and their accomplices), while also applying to those who stood up to protect the world against the repetition of such heinous crimes.

None can deny that there is a strong moral argument behind the claim, that those who fight terrorism should not be bound by the same rules as apply to the terrorists and their supporters; and, indeed, this is valid at the national level. However, we must keep in mind that there is no universally accepted definition of terrorism at the international level. Accepting that humanitarian law does not apply to the fight against terror, even when this fight takes the form of an armed conflict, it would seriously breach the dyke of humanitarian protection. Abuse will soon engulf the breach. The inevitable result would be that warring parties would deny their prisoners the benefit of humanitarian protection, on the grounds that they were 'terrorists'.

Whatever the strength of the moral argument, the law in force must nevertheless be respected. The members of the Grand Alliance that fought Nazi Germany were certainly well aware that they were battling the most criminal of regimes. To the best of my knowledge, however, there was never any doubt – at least for the British and US governments – that humanitarian law applied to their relations with Germany.

It has been accepted for centuries that the application of the laws of armed conflict does not depend on the nature or the origin of the conflict, nor on the causes espoused by the parties to it. The wounded and sick must be collected and cared for, prisoners must be respected, the civilian population must be spared the effects of the hostilities and protected from ill-treatment, whatever side they are on. Any other approach will lead to the collapse of the system of legal protection, with each belligerent claiming that its cause is just and using this claim as an argument to deny humanitarian protection to its adversaries. Inasmuch as 'the war against terror' implies the use of military force and leads to armed conflict, there is no doubt that such operations are ruled by the law of armed conflict. Humanitarian values must be respected, even in the war against terrorism.

This does not mean that humanitarian law as it stands is perfect or that it perfectly fits the new environment. Humanitarian rules, like any body of law, are drafted by human beings and can be revised or improved.

So far, the International Committee of the Red Cross, which has a mandate to 'work for the faithful application of international humanitarian law' and 'prepare any development thereof', has not taken any decision concerning possible developments of existing law, nor has it received any formal proposal to that effect. However, thinking aloud and based on some 30 years of experience in the humanitarian field, I might venture to suggest some ideas that could be explored in this respect.

First of all, from a methodological point of view, we should refrain from drafting new proposals in response exclusively to the events of 11 September 2001. Whether at the national or the international level, new rules should not be drafted in response to a single event, however dramatic. Such rules would be bound to be outdated by the time they were adopted, since history never repeats itself word for word. We should therefore analyse recent conflicts so as to identify general trends and draft new rules in response to them.

Secondly, the causes of any shortcoming should be clearly identified. If atrocities have taken place, was it because the perpetrators exploited loopholes in existing rules, or was it because existing rules were not respected? If the law was inadequate, new codification may be the proper response. If existing law was not complied with, the response should consist of diplomatic or political action rather than new codification. What would be the use of new rules if the problem arises from the rules already in force being disregarded?

In term of substance, several questions should be addressed.

First of all, we may question the relevance of the distinction between international and non-international armed conflict on which humanitarian law is based. As you know, the Geneva Conventions and Additional Protocol I apply *ipso jure* to international armed conflicts, while only the minimal provisions incorporated in Article 3, common to all four

Geneva Conventions and Additional Protocol II, apply to non-international conflicts. In practice, however, we are often confronted with situations where the two overlap. The recent conflict in Afghanistan is a case in point: as of 7 October 2001, the international armed conflict between the United States and Britain on one side and the Taliban on the other, suddenly overshadowed a non-international armed conflict between the Taliban and the Northern Alliance, which had been going on since 1996. Highly respected scholars have suggested dropping the distinction between the two forms of conflict.

This proposal is appealing. We must nevertheless bear in mind that the distinction between international and non-international armed conflict is rooted in the very concept of state sovereignty as applied to the law of armed conflict. It is therefore doubtful that the states will be prepared to abandon it, even though they do in practice, apply to non-international armed conflicts part of the rules developed for international conflicts.

Another approach – in my view more promising – would be to develop the law applicable to non-international armed conflict so as progressively to bridge the gap between the two sets of rules. The study on customary international humanitarian law, which the International Committee of the Red Cross has carried out with the support of a group of leading international experts, shows that the rules governing the conduct of hostilities, as set out in Additional Protocol I of 8 June 1977, reflect customary international law, and that such rules apply to international and non-international armed conflicts alike.

The recent decision to extend to non-international armed conflicts the field of application of the 1980 Convention on certain conventional weapons indicates that such developments are today possible. It points out a direction that might be usefully explored in respect to other rules. In this connection, I would like to pay special tribute to the governments of the United Kingdom and Canada, which have already ratified the revised Convention adopted last December. I hope that this example will soon be followed by other States.

Should there be agreement to develop the body of rules applicable to non-international armed conflicts, a thorny issue which might have to be addressed is whether some mechanism should not be devised that would allow non-state entities to express their commitment to respecting the rules applicable to non-international armed conflicts. Needless to say, it might be objected that non-state actors could easily misuse such a mechanism to acquire some form of international status without any serious intention of respecting the law. That risk exists, but the same may obviously be true for states. On the other hand, it may be illusory to expect that non-state entities will abide by humanitarian rules unless they are given the means to express their commitment to do so. Furthermore, Article 3, common to all four Geneva Conventions, expressly stipulates that the application of [its] provisions shall not affect the legal status of the parties to the conflict. The same provision could be part of any new mechanism that would allow non-state actors to express their commitment to comply with humanitarian rules.

A third direction to be explored would be the adoption of some form of 'humanitarian safety net' that would provide fundamental humanitarian guaranties and would apply to any person in any armed conflict. This net would protect all those who do not benefit from a more favourable status. We too often observe that war victims are denied the benefit of the humanitarian regimes established to protect them, for reasons arising either from the nature of the conflict, or from their personal situation. Such a safety net would protect all against abuse and arbitrary treatment.

The objection could be made that Article 75 of Additional Protocol I already sets out fundamental guarantees which apply to those not entitled to more favourable treatment under the Geneva Conventions or the Protocol. However, as part of Protocol I, this provision applies only to international armed conflicts. What is needed is catch-all humanitarian rules applicable in all circumstances.

No rule is worth the paper it is printed on unless it is actually implemented. With respect to recent conflicts, there has been a general feeling that substantive rules did indeed exist but that major crimes nevertheless occurred owing to utter failure to respect those rules. Special consideration should therefore be given to strengthening the mechanisms for ensuring the law's implementation.

Preventive action is a key factor. Humanitarian law cannot be complied with unless the officers and soldiers who have this obligation know about it and have been trained to respect it. Hence the importance of integrating humanitarian law into military training programmes and operational procedures. Similarly, national legislation should be adapted to ensure that it tallies with international obligations.

With the setting up of the international tribunals for the former Yugoslavia, Rwanda and Sierra Leone, and even more conspicuously with the adoption of the Rome Statute of the International Criminal Court, the international community has taken major steps to ensure that breaches of international humanitarian law are repressed. Besides restoring the authority of the law and punishing violators, it is expected that these measures will exert a strong deterrent effect on future violators since they will know that they might be held accountable for their deeds.

Where new developments might be needed is in the realm between prevention and repression, in the field of ongoing scrutiny, either by strengthening the powers of the International Committee of the Red Cross – which has a mandate 'to endeavour at all times to ensure the protection of and assistance to the victims of armed conflict', but which has only limited means at its disposal to do so – or by creating some new mechanism, such as a corps of international observers, as suggested on behalf of the European Union during the Conference on compliance with the Fourth Geneva Convention in the territories occupied by Israel, held on 5 December 2001.

It is also possible to imagine some kind of diplomatic mechanism to iron out differences and ensure greater respect for humanitarian law. Since major differences often arise from differing legal analysis of conflicts and of the law applicable to them, states could apply to the International Court of Justice to rule on these matters.

While considering possible developments of existing rules, we must take care not to jeopardize the legal regime established by the Geneva Conventions and Additional Protocols. The objective of any new codification should therefore be the adoption of an additional protocol, rather than a revision of the Conventions now in force.

Whatever direction is taken, however, one fundamental issue will have to be addressed. Whereas humanitarian law is ultimately based on the assumption that both States and non-state entities claiming to exercise public authority are willing to abide by its fundamental tenets, we are now confronted with a world in which some countries openly reject fundamental humanitarian rules and principles outright. This is the case when an organization sets out to attack American interests and citizens, wherever they may be found. Is it reasonable to expect that states fighting such an organization will abide by humanitarian rules, when they know that their adversaries not only will fail to respect them, but openly reject such rules?

Obviously, there is no straightforward solution to this. What can be said, however, is that no terrorist organization can, by its own means, subvert a modern democratic state that functions according to the rule of law, government based on the consent of the governed and respect for basic human rights and fundamental freedoms. As far as is known, terrorist leaders realize this and expect that the trauma caused by their aggression will lead the state affected to react in such a way, as to undermine the moral values on which it is based.

More conspicuously, we must bear in mind that if liberal societies have accepted high moral standards, it is not primarily for the sake of their enemies, but for themselves. We know that there are sometimes situations where we have to stand up and fight to preserve the moral values that are dear to our hearts. We must ensure that the weapons we use to protect those moral values do not in fact endanger them.

Discussion

Middle East

There is uncertainty about a definition of the expression 'use of force', whether violence has actually been delivered or other coercive means used. The 'actual use' of military violence is the normal legal definition, but the threat to use force is prohibited also by Article 24 of the UN Charter. This is not the same, however, as the concept of taking pre-emptive action for the purpose of self-defence, under threat of an imminent attack. Having overwhelming (disproportionate) means of retaliation against an attack, such as the possession of nuclear weapons, is not overtly a 'threat' of force. Demand for regime change, by indicating imminent use of force, clearly is a threat and is disallowed under Article 24. It is important that just war doctrine and the use of military force do not permit acts of revenge or punishment. Likewise no Security Council Resolution (SCR) has ever mentioned 'assassination' or justification for it.

A Security Council Resolution is desirable before force can be used, but is not always necessary, for example in the case of previous SCRs being ignored by Iraq. A fresh SCR would, however, put the matter beyond further doubt and show self-defence as justification. Under mandate of the UN Security Council, however, a Resolution to enable force to be used is not *carte blanche*. The duty of all parties is to comply with the Geneva Convention and other rules and laws of wars. The SCR offers no protection to parties infringing the requirements of *jus in bello*. Nations on the Security Council can of course veto SCRs for political purposes, which complicates how much force is permissible. There are at least two other sets of proceedings being considered currently by the International Court of Justice, arguing different moral and legal standpoints for the justification for the use of force. The Christian just war tradition is one of a number of such considerations.

A clear historical illustration of the unlawful use of force was the Iraqi invasion of Iran in 1980, which was just as blatant a violation of international law as the Iraqi invasion of Kuwait in 1990. Ignoring legal issues on grounds of *Realpolitik* has a high price, since so many of us took no notice of the former. Dwelling on other security matters in the region, Iran undoubtedly feels threatened in respect of Israel's recent expressed intention to 'take out' the Iranian nuclear reactors, as they demonstrated in taking out the Iraqi's nuclear facility in 1982. However, the Iranian justification for allocating Israel to meet this threat is dubious because the threat is more general than imminent. The Iranian Ministry of Defence would have to ask itself whether Iran's security would be better protected the day after an air strike against Israel than the day before. It is doubtful. The critical test of 'necessity' would not be met.

'Regime change' is a convenient term that nonetheless will bedevil the legality and practicality of what is happening for years to come. Changing a regime cannot be justification in itself for the use of force. Regime change may be a necessary part of the process of achieving the goal one is entitled to achieve, such as enforcing a Security Council Resolution, securing self-defence or securing humanitarian intervention. Ironically, in 1987 the West went to the brink of using force against Iran, because Iran was saying it had to secure regime change in Baghdad.

If one is comparing SCRs raised against Israel, we discover that only one SCR is binding on Israel: of those raised against Iraq *all* are binding, with one exception. This is a legal point that is significant. The far more important practical difference is that SCR 242 calls on the Arab States and Palestine Liberation Organization on the one side and Israel on the other to take certain actions. The US and others manifestly have not tried to enforce this SCR against Israel, nor has any nation tried to enforce it against the Arab States either. The moral and legal position of SCR 678 was clearer. Kuwait was legally blameless at the time of the Iraqi invasion in 1990. One could not say by the same token that either the Arabs on one hand, or the Israelis on the other, were blameless in the war of 1967. Resolutions about Western Sahara and East Timor are not in the same league as SCRs 242 and 678.

Prisoners

Turning to the question of prisoner of war status, and using terminology of 'war' and 'conflict', any doubts about the status of Vietcong prisoners of war held by US or South Vietnamese troops, could only legally have been questioned by those individuals not 'distinguishing' themselves (such as wearing army uniforms) from the civilian population. Likewise, North

Vietnamese claims that US captives were not POWs because they were 'aggressors' was wholly unjustified.

Arguably the status of captives held in the US base at Guantanamo Bay, Cuba remains uncertain. There should be no territory anywhere that is not subject to the jurisdiction of a nation state, with ordinary domestic safeguards for prisoners, including in this case, access to legal representation either under Cuban law or US law. The International Committee of the Red Cross (ICRC) believes that members of the former armed forces of Afghanistan held by US and other authorities should, as a minimum presumption, be awarded POW status. Others, captured under different circumstances and coming from many other countries, should have their status decided by a competent tribunal, under the provision of Article 5 of the Third Geneva Convention. Individual situations should be addressed individually, not collectively. If any individuals have committed actual crimes, they should be prosecuted, tried under law and their fate be properly determined. Others who cannot be charged with crimes will have to be returned to their country of origin.

There remains, of course, doubt that the international conflict in Afghanistan has come to an end. Those released may indeed present a continuing threat, but continuing custody or release should, in the ICRC's view, be a matter of legal determination, not administrative convenience. Furthermore, the ICRC believes that either Cuban or US jurisdiction must apply, but that US courts have jurisdiction regarding acts that take place on US soil, US vessels or even in the Guantanamo base itself. Undoubtedly, since the 1990-1991 conflict with Iraq is not over, the Geneva Conventions still apply, as do the sanctions enforced by the UN. This state of 'ceasefire', rather than peace treaty, is far from satisfactory. Recognizing that there are such people as illegal combatants, the ICRC nevertheless believes that both POWs and civilians should *always* be protected by the Geneva Conventions and International Humanitarian Law.

Chapter 3

The Moral High Ground

Strategies for Engaging Secessionary Conflicts

Marc Weller

It is very dangerous to ask an international lawyer about morality. This is not because lawyers tend to be devoid of morality, but because sometimes we try to divide the two. However, there are of course so many issues that converge in public debate – legal issues, moral issues, sometimes even religious precepts. In terms of 'just war' doctrine, it is interesting that, after almost a hundred years of the development of international legal rules, we find that sometimes we are addressing, although in a slightly different language, the very same issues that philosophers have been addressing, that religious experts have been addressing, or indeed that lawyers have been addressing for a very long time.

There has been mention of 'proportionality' and what are grounds for humanitarian intervention. The question has been posed; are there reasons for preventative or pre-emptive wars? Issues that we thought had receded into the dark and distant background since 1945 quite suddenly become headline news almost every day. Such instances are when we discuss the application of a doctrine of preventative war in relation to Iraq; or the central role of the United Nations in relation to authorization concerning the use of force; or when we return to a reliance on traditional views on self-defence; or are faced with situations such as the terrorism of an armed attack which we saw on 11 September 2001.

How do we encompass and reasonably address these kinds of phenomena, which have developed since 1945, within legal rules and doctrines, and the UN framework based on a new and different set of circumstances?

Marc Weller is Assistant Director of Studies at the Centre for International Studies, University of Cambridge. He has been visiting Professor and Lecturer variously at the Universities of Paris, King's College London and the Estonian Diplomatic Academy. He has served as Counsel representing the Government of Bosnia and Herzegovina and is the Director of the European Centre for Minority Issues.

I shall dwell particularly on those factors that form the background to the discussion of asymmetrical warfare: the idea that on the one hand you have a privileged government that has control over the state including the military, and on the other hand you have an entity that claims legitimacy for the use of force either against that government, or, perhaps if it cannot attack the government, it attacks others in order to make its political case.

We are all focused on the situation in Iraq, and the issue of counter-terrorism operations in relation to Al-Qa'ida in Afghanistan and a number of other issues that remain unresolved. In order to make our legal framework fit these new kinds of facts, we need to ensure that a framework of some sort remains in place, ensuring that the use of force remains limited and well-targeted towards legitimate and proportionate aims. But let us not forget that, in principle, it has been clear since 1945 and certainly since the end of the Cold War that the vast majority of conflicts around the world have tended to be *internal* armed conflicts. The vast majority of casualties, with the exceptions perhaps of Iran, Iraq, Ethiopia and Eritrea, have occurred in devastating and very damaging internal armed confrontations.

There are no more violent and no more long-term confrontations than those that arise from 'self-determination conflicts'. If you were to name some of the conflicts of this type, you will find that quite a few of them actually have a history of armed violence and use of force that goes back continually over half a century. For example, the internal armed conflicts in Myanmar (Burma) and Kashmir never seem to be resolved or being near to resolution. Such strife has had a tremendous direct impact on their own societies, but some conflicts about self-determination (for example in Palestine) have also had an impact in the wider region or even globally.

As our topic is about asymmetric warfare, it might be useful to address why it is that self-determination conflicts almost invariably result in armed struggle. Secondly, we need to consider how the international legal system has classically balanced the interest of the international system and central governments against the interests of those struggling for secession, for self-determination as they see it. Then we need to see whether during the 1990s there have been some changes to the doctrines that are applied in these contexts. Finally we must see whether we have managed actually to address, through concerted international action, the causes and ways to resolve some of these conflicts. I can report to you that the revival of doctrines, which most of us had consigned to the dustbin of history, such as armed reprisals and preventative wars to counter disconcerting developments, together with the problems of asymmetrical hostilities and self-determination conflicts, have helped to achieve some great advances in recent years.

In explaining why it is that self-determination conflicts tend, by definition, to be asymmetrical, the answer is quite simple. The very structure of the international system is one which is constructed, defined and developed by governments acting together as the so-called organized international community of states. They create the basic rules that govern that system. It is therefore not surprising that governments have ensured, in the way they have set up the system, that their position is uniquely privileged over that of other actors, in particular of course non-state actors. Therefore, where you have internal armed conflicts, including self-determination conflicts, you will normally find a situation whereby a government is legally privileged, entitled to use force against those who wish to challenge the status quo and entitled to receive international assistance in this campaign, whereas those who struggle against the government are declared 'bandits', 'rebels', even 'the terrorists'.

There is one exception where the situation is radically reversed, and that is when a group, struggling against a state, can claim and persuade others that they are indeed a 'self-determination movement', and the international system ensures that the government no longer will win the conflict. The government is thereby legally obliged to cease to use repressive measures against the movement, and must in a sense give up the fight. If it continues to use force, that movement may continue the struggle and even receive external assistance. So the doctrine of self-determination, where it applies, is an extraordinarily vigorous, decisive fact. If it applies against governments, it reverses the privilege that governments normally exercise and enjoy over non-governmental entities.

A sentence more dangerous than the following one has hardly ever been uttered. It is a quotation from a judge in the International Court of Justice, who dealt with a self-determination case some decades ago. He said, 'It is for the people to determine the destiny of a territory and not for a territory to determine the destiny of a people'. The moral high ground which the judge took then resonates well in the jungles of North Eastern Sri Lanka and in other places where people reach for their Kalashnikov rifle and say, 'Aha! It is for us to determine and shape the destiny of our territory through a struggle for self-determination; we are entitled to do this'.

Of course this situation is one of grave confusion. Much of the discourse and the conflicts over the last ten years have been based on the misunderstanding of who is entitled to benefit from this extraordinarily powerful doctrine of self-determination, if it applies. Now that the decolonization process has virtually been completed it applies to no single entity now, and the only examples that are left are Palestine and Western Sahara. The claim in East Timor, a genuine colonial self-determination entity, has now finally been resolved. Other entities enjoy self-determination in the sense that they should be part of democratically governed state constitutions. Human Rights should be dominant. Self-determination might imply that minorities ought to enjoy minority rights, while other groups ought to have collective rights representing their identity. But this extraordinary, vigorous and possibly violent right of self-determination, which the international legal system has accepted, has of course only been accepted in the narrow circumstances of an anti-colonial struggle. A historic wrong of such magnitude that persuades the member states of the United Nations to accept that a non-state entity under discussion can obtain unilateral secession, if necessary through a struggle, is nevertheless still disputed. Most governments may accept the necessity of the struggle, but not the United Kingdom and the United States.

The problem is that entities that do not qualify under this extremely narrow definition of self-determination have no remedy to seek their interest or represent their identity *vis à vis* the central state. Of course there can always be a secession or independence of an entity if the central government agrees, but very rarely will it do so. We have the example of the dissolution of the USSR, and the agreed secession of Eritrea, but only after quite violent ruptures of the Soviet and Ethiopian governmental structures. Otherwise governments of course will not normally be keen to agree to a secession: self-determination is traditionally defined as an 'all or nothing' doctrine. Either the claimant becomes fully independent as a state, or the central state retains sovereignty and exercises absolute power over the claimant. Speaking somewhat in the abstract, we are not really referring to 'absolute power'. Conceptually we mean the unique source of 'state authority', from which any powers enjoyed by subordinate entities, such as provinces or other dependent parts of territory, are derived.

Since 1990, and the end of the Cold War, we have happily seen some extraordinary attempts to overcome this 'all or nothing' deadlock. A number of settlements have been adopted around the world in relation to what previously appeared to be irresolvable self-determination conflicts. I must confess a number of unaddressed conflicts of this kind still exist, Kashmir being one such example, although until a few years ago even there a glimmer of hope existed that a solution could be found.

Now let me very briefly invite you to consider two or three aspects of this important change that has occurred and allows us to remove the perceptions of entities that *think* they are self-determination units, and have an entitlement to be states, but still must not use force. The first aspect relates to the flexibility of dealing with claims to self-determination on their own terms. There are three strategies that we have recently observed, when attempts are made to deal with these asymmetrical conflicts. One has been to try and persuade the secessionist entity to rejoin the state. In a sense this is a constitutional, not primarily an international legal act of reconstituting the state. The act is one of freely opting into the state. A new type of state would be formed in which there would be a changed constitutional structure, which can either be one that grants autonomy to the entity seeking change (having previously sought change through violence), or it can be a looser, federal-type structure, which the states opt into. I was involved in a number of negotiations of this kind, where the absolute crucial issue was that the entity that was previously struggling forcibly for what it *thought* was its right of formal self-determination and then state 'from our perspective we are now acting on our right of self-determination and doing it by opting into this new state. At this point in time our right of self-determination expires, because we have now exercised it by joining this new constitutional consensus'.

A solution was found with respect to the armed insurgency of the Taureg in Mali. An internal solution has been attempted at least by the French in relation to Corsican constitutional reform. A solution that has been attempted in Gagauzia, a large territory within Moldova, which opted in through an act of self-determination and obtained in the new Moldavian constitution for the first time an acknowledgement of its entitlement to a somewhat separate status. Should Moldova ever change its own status of being an independent state and join another state, the consequences for Gagauzia would be very interesting. We have seen attempts in Georgia to perform something similar, although there we only had 'agreements to come to an agreement', which thus far, unfortunately, has not been implemented. We have achieved agreement in Milanou, where the agreement of 1996 has actually become an autonomy arrangement, whereby power is handed over to the formerly-armed rebels.

That is an extraordinarily satisfying thing to witness in one sense, namely that where those who have previously used violence against that state can feel confident in a new larger entity, and subsequently join the consensus on forming a new state. But also we have sometimes witnessed the adopted solution, being that of handing over power to the rebel movement that had previously fought against the state. The conflict is then simply forgotten. I emphasize this because I have peripherally been involved in attempts to negotiate a solution relating to Sri Lanka, which as you know continues at this very minute. There has been a temptation to say 'The Tamil Tigers are so vigorous and dangerous, we now really need peace and want peace'. In addition to having an autonomy arrangement which is the right solution, one forgets to attach to this arrangement a mechanism by which the power that is to be exercised within the newly autonomous entity and needs to be grounded on some sort of popular consensus. If not, new minorities that find themselves suddenly trapped within this autonomous or virtually independent entity may not be fully protected. This is the very situation of the Muslim population in the North Eastern provinces of Sri Lanka.

The second option is an interim option, where one says, 'we are not going to prejudice what happens in the end'. It may well be that the central government, through this peace agreement, now accepts a new constitution, assigning to the formerly-secessionist unit a new constitutional right of self-determination. We must not forget that the international legal right to wage war in an anti-colonial struggle does *not* apply. Instead of resorting to force, the parties agree to reconstitute the state so that the entity has a constitutional entitlement to decide, at a later stage, to continue to be part of the state or to leave. Constitutional self-determination was initially attempted in Chechnya in the 1996 Limited Agreement, when Chechnya was promised that after three years the consensus for self-determination would be measured. It was not a successful agreement in the end, as the Russian government, which asserted that Chechen rebels had engaged in terrorism operations in Moscow, unilaterally abrogated it. This indicates how important it is to have an agreement that is internationally recognized, and one that cannot be subject to the change of heart of one or the other parties, at least not too easily.

There are several different types of agreements for reformulating a state and perhaps, in some instances, allowing for the possibility of independence. Bosnia is an example of the fundamental reconstruction of a state that does not grant independence beyond federated autonomy. There we have a 'reconstition', where it was absolutely essential that it would not include a separate identity for any of the constituent units, to the extent that they could go their separate ways after an interim period. SUBSCA may have special relations with external states, say Serbia or Yugoslavia, but it cannot secede. Another example is the position of Serbia and Montenegro, who are now negotiating a new constitution under an EU-mediated agreement. It is clear that, after a three-year period, any entity that wishes to can actually leave. That is less surprising because, from the beginning, it was clear that Montenegro actually has a constitutional right of self-determination, as had the other Yugoslav republics.

There are other interim solutions that avoid the issue of self-determination for the moment. Kosovo is the best example. Resolution 1244 of the UN Security Council confirms the territorial integrity of Yugoslavia, including Kosovo, which was also recently confirmed by the Serbian Montenegro Agreement (2002) and ratified in a way by the Security Council. But on the other hand, Resolution 1244 also refers back to the Rambouillet Agreement (1999) that was also ratified by the Security Council. Those agreements provided for a mechanism to work out a final status and settlement for Kosovo. This shows a dual system. In the Northern Ireland Agreements (1998), the package that clarifies the identity of the self-determination entity and also how a constitutional claim of self-determination could be addressed in the future allows for a referendum, but only in Northern Ireland itself. The hope is that, over time, the need to exercise the possibility of a referendum will recede once the participants in the settlement realize that there is no longer the question of sovereignty being exclusively located in Point A or Point B. A complex arrangement has been generated, whereby location does not really matter. Ultimately, sovereignty lies where authority is best exercised, be it by local government, or be it internationalized governments, in this case including those of the Republic of Ireland, the United Kingdom and Northern Irish Authorities.

The fascinating recent example of Bougainville, where it is agreed by Papua New Guinea that, after ten to fifteen years, if Bougainville behaves according to the 'criteria' for good behaviour, part of the agreement will enable a referendum. The outcome of the referendum might be either self-determination or secession. After a period of very violent conflict, the people of Bougainville seem to be jubilant, feeling that there is no longer the need to struggle or use force to claim their self-determination. They believe 'independence' has been achieved, whereas the Papua-New Guinean government hopes that after ten to fifteen years the Bougainvillians will have administered themselves autonomously and they will have realized that the benefits of a continued association with a larger state far outweighs any irrational attempt to be entirely separate'. The criteria for the exercise of the referendum may be clear, but who determines whether they have been fulfilled remains unclear.

The final type of settlement involves accepting at the outset that the entity can become a state, such as in the case of Eritrea, in which the government agreed to let the entity go after an interim period of two years or so, if supported by a referendum. In the case of the Sudan, under the Machakos Protocol (2002), the Sudanese government has agreed that, after an interim period of six years, the South can hold a referendum on independence. However, the latest rounds of negotiation (Machakos II), which seemed very close to being successful, now seems to be in a state of collapse, or have just been interrupted only in relation to the Sudan. The Sudanese government may think that after six years of exploiting joint areas of oil exportation and other interests, the South might no longer wish to leave. The Southern rebels may believe themselves virtually independent at this stage, having obtained their concession.

Therefore there has been a considerable application of new ideas and different ways of getting to grips with the crux of the self-determination issue. I can only mention the other, second phenomenon in passing. That is the fantasy that is now being put to work when conceiving new models of 'co-governance' within states. That is the attempt to find a middle way and avoid a situation in which an entity is either fully independent and has all authority, or is entirely subjected to a central government. Witness the unhelpful experience of the Bosnia Settlement, where a number of mechanisms were tried which do not really work, although double and triple safeguards for this or that community had been devised.

We have also seen recently in the example of the Macedonian Settlement that a violent armed conflict that was about to break out could be stopped through a political settlement. It seemed to satisfy the protagonists of this armed conflict to an extent that they were willing to give up their arms and hand them over – well at least some of them – to NATO. There are some other very cunning ways of power-sharing, combining several methods and means.

A crucial battle has been won for all of us interested in international stability, by deliberately rejecting an attempt by armed violent self-determination movements to be dignified with the label of genuine post-colonial self-determination, and therefore being entitled to statehood through the use of force. Many thought that the Yugoslav conflict would have opened the door towards even wider-ranging claims of independence through the use of force. But in the two examples of Kosovo and Northern Ireland we have seen that, at least thus far, the international community has insisted that intervention operations be launched to protect the entity from grave humanitarian violations, but only on the condition that it does not use the opportunity to secede unilaterally. Instead we have seen that another doctrine has been invented, that of 'constitutionally agreed self-determination', where statehood could be the end result, but not always necessarily, as a number of other options are available. We have seen that options short of statehood have, in a number of instances, terminated very vicious and violent armed conflicts. We are now seeing that interim arrangements of extraordinary complexity are being applied. There is now a body of understanding and advice on how to avoid some of the mistakes of the early history of the development of legal and political concepts, thereby reducing the likelihood of the use of force. We can study these cases fruitfully, particularly if we wish to avoid being drawn into asymmetrical warfare.

Nations Hosting International Terrorists and Criminals: the Moral, Legal and Military Vulnerability

Pierre-Richard Prosper

The essence of my subject is that states that host terrorists and international criminals must, in so doing, accept the moral and legal obligations and consequences. There is much to study and discuss on this subject.

We find ourselves at a critical time in history, a time when the rule of law is being severely challenged by those who seek to defy it and wreak havoc around the world. The challenge before us is to combat these forces of lawlessness and evil, striving to build what I would call 'an international web of justice', in order to spread the rule of law, to end 'cultures of impunity' and ensure that violators of international humanitarian law are held to account. While clearly we note today that there is a tremendous amount to debate about the best approach, I think we all agree that we have the same goal in mind.

To get a full appreciation of what we are dealing with, I think it is best to address the present circumstances. To understand them we must look back to a year ago, to September 2001, when we learned the painful lesson of how lawlessness in the most remote corners of our world can, indeed, be a threat to civilization throughout the world.

On 11 September, terrorists attacked civilization itself. We saw an event where citizens of more than ninety countries were killed in the concentrated attacks, which proved to be much more than isolated or sporadic acts of violence. Al-Qa'ida, a foreign, private, terrorist network, issued a declaration of war against the United States, against our allies, against civilization. This was a group that organized, campaigned and trained over the course of years to commit cowardly, indiscriminate and unprecedent-

---

Ambassador Pierre-Richard Prosper is US Ambassador-at-Large for War Crimes Issues. From 1996-98 he was lead prosecutor at the United Nations International Criminal Tribunal for Rwanda, and in the US investigated and prosecuted major international drug cartels. In 2000-2001, he was Wasserstein Fellow at Harvard Law School.

ed attacks of violence and terror. Al-Qa'ida history is filled with a decade's worth of hostile rhetoric and directives to kill civilians. We know they were responsible for the first bombing of the World Trade Center in 1993, linked to the attacks of US service members in Somalia in 1993 and responsible for the bombing of the US embassies in Nairobi and Dar-es-Salaam and the attack on the USS *Cole*. We also know that the evidence is undisputed that this group perpetrated the horrifying and unprovoked air assaults on the World Trade Center, the Pentagon and of course the tragedy in Pennsylvania. Their 'campaign of terror' continues even today.

At a time when the world is experiencing a growth of democratic ideals and strengthening of freedom, the threats that we face have spread in unprecedented ways and are becoming even more menacing. We now find ourselves faced with an unconventional war, fought by unconventional means. Today the threat is not just from states that would subvert peace and international law, murdering innocent lives and seeking to augment their power and control. Today we face private organizations whose disregard for human life and the rule of the law increasingly crosses international boundaries, impacting on all of us.

The United States believes that it is imperative that the international community comes together and works more closely than ever before, to prevent such indiscriminate and unconventional methods of warfare and utter disregard for well-established principles of international law. In order to be successful in combating this evil, all states must recognise and accept their moral, legal and military obligations and responsibilities. States must guard against those who commit war crimes, crimes against humanity, and other atrocities against civilization itself. We must strive to bring the perpetrators to justice.

After 11 September 2001, the international community gathered in New York in the United Nations and called for proactive measures to stop the illegal targeting of civilians. The Security Council used its Chapter 7 authority to pass sweeping and innovative resolutions that obliged all states to work together for one common objective: to prevent and suppress terrorist acts, through increased cooperation and full implementation of relevant international conventions relating to terrorism. We believe that these resolutions are our tools. They lay out the responsibilities and detail the obligations. With states using their unilateral authority and unilateral power, we believe that the reach of law is thereby extended and strengthened, to combat these abuses. After 11 September we saw a coalition being formed: it was created by legal authority under Security Council

Resolution 1373, which requires states to ensure that any person who participates in the financing, planning, preparation or support of terrorist acts are to be brought to justice. The resolution also imposes a duty on states to establish terrorist acts as serious criminal offences in domestic law, backed by punishments that reflect the gravity of the acts. It requires states to deny a safe haven and improve international efforts to restrict financial support for terrorist organizations.

Now as a result of this broad-based initiative, we have seen what can be achieved when the international community comes together and forms a coalition to combat abuses and to fight those who would commit and sponsor atrocities. We are witnessing success. Most notably, we can look to the situation in Afghanistan. We can assert that Afghanistan is no longer under the control of a brutal Taliban regime. The Al-Qa'ida network there is being dismantled: its support and protection in the territory is rapidly diminishing. The citizens of Afghanistan are now free to live their lives without, for instance, the terrible oppression of women. This is the result of the combined effort of over 16 000 troops from twenty nations, directly supporting military operations. As we know, foreign assistance has started to flow. Within the last year, for example, the United States has provided $420 million for reconstruction in Afghanistan and delivered enough food to feed six million people for at least seven months. An effective interim government, committed to holding fair and free elections and promoting democratic values, has begun to develop. Given this more stable environment, over 1.5 million refuges have returned home this year.

Globally, we are seeing the progress of coalitions fighting terror as a result of Security Council Resolution 1373. Over ninety nations, stretching from Spain to Singapore, have arrested or detained more than 2 400 terrorists since the passing of the Resolution. More than 160 nations have frozen over $116 million of assets associated with terrorist groups and their supporters. We believe that it is this type of collective effort that is needed to correct the course of history and to improve the situation for humanity. The obligation of states to combat war crimes, terrorism and other threats to international peace and security is now clear. States must fulfil their obligations to the international community, or risk becoming vulnerable to severe and serious consequences, such as further bloodshed or instability throughout their region. They may even need to take military action, exercising their right to anticipatory or collective self-defence under the UN Charter.

While much of the discussion today is on terrorism, I must point out that it is also crucial that we pursue other types of international criminals, particularly those who spread terror and lawlessness in perpetrating genocide, crimes against humanity and war crimes, regardless of where it occurs. We believe that we are making progress on that front as well. By placing the responsibility where it belongs, back on the states, war criminals as well as terrorists are being apprehended and held accountable for their crimes. In Africa and the Balkans more fugitives wanted for war crimes were brought into custody last year than in the previous two years combined. A total of forty-four persons were indicted by the Tribunal for Yugoslavia and the Tribunal for Rwanda. For example, in September 2002 in the Great Lakes region one of the accused leaders of the Rwandan genocide, a 'most wanted person' by the name of Jean-Baptiste Gatete was apprehended by the Republic of the Congo and transferred to the Tribunal. In August 2002 in Angola, General Augustine Bizimungo, another 'most wanted criminal' responsible for Rwandan genocide was apprehended. Both of these fugitives were the key targets of our Rewards for Justice Program, which offers up to $5 million for information leading to their arrest. In the coming weeks, we expect to see more arrests throughout the African continent, particularly the Great Lakes region, in Brazzaville (Republic of Congo) and Kinshasa (Democratic Republic of Congo). It is clear that states in the region are starting to understand their responsibility for taking proactive measures, acting to apprehend and arrest those that are bent on abuse of human rights, thereby ensuring peace and stability.

In the Balkans we have also seen changes whereby a pattern of cooperation is now developing in Serbia, Bosnia and Croatia, as part of the work of the International War Crimes Tribunal in the Hague. There is also a new movement towards more domestic prosecution, which we believe will extend the reach of the law. The states are now working on legislation designed to end impunity and restore basic moral values of humanity. Of course we recognise that, in order to seek true success in that region, Radovan Karadzic and Radko Mladic in particular must be brought swiftly to justice.

But I cannot talk about international peace, stability, accountability and atrocities without discussing the issue of the day, and that is Iraq. In my work as Ambassador at Large for War Crimes Issues, I find myself repeatedly pressing governments around the world to cooperate fully with international instruments and international norms. I frequently cite the UN Charter, UN Security Council Resolutions and seek the apprehension of those who are committing atrocities and abusing their population. As part of our policy, we back up our message and rhetoric with economic and political consequences. We feel that this is our duty and responsibility. We believe that if we were to insist on compliance, then we must be prepared to enforce it. But with Iraq, international law and the consensus of the international community has been repeatedly ignored, thwarted and defied. As President Bush asserted to the General Assembly (12 September 2002), in reference to the Iraqi regime's stated commitment to destroy and stop developing weapons of mass destruction, Iraq has broken every aspect of that fundamental pledge. Today we know that Saddam Hussein is continuing to violate sixteen UN Security Council Resolutions and at least thirty United Nations Security Council Presidential Statements. President Bush confirms that in his quest to seek and create weapons of mass destruction Hussein poses a grave and gathering danger for the international community. We believe this threat must be addressed for the benefit of the present and future generations.

To understand the threat, we need only to look at the past, we need only to look at the deeds of Saddam Hussein, to know that his willingness to commit atrocities and use weapons of mass destruction is large. Reports of his past actions and atrocities read like an indictment. From the beginning of his career as Chief of Iraqi Security Services in 1968, Saddam is alleged to have executed potential rivals, including scores of high level government officials and thousands of political prisoners. As President he has stopped at nothing to preserve his personal power and the survival of his regime.

Since the 1970s he has escalated, and made routine, the systematic torture and execution of political prisoners. There is evidence that he ordered the use of chemical weapons against the Iranian forces in the 1980-1988 Iran-Iraq War. But Iraq's campaign of the 1980s, against the predominantly Kurdish civilians in Northern Iraq, was probably his most brutal and most violent acts, resulting in the death of up to 100 000 people, according to the independent organization Human Rights Watch. We know in that period, over 4 000 villages were destroyed forty gas attacks were launched against the Kurdish villagers, including the largest attack in 1988 at Halabja that caused 3 500-5 000 casualties, again according to Human Rights Watch. The chemical agents used were mustard gas and nerve gases. In 1991 Saddam directed the bloody suppression of the Kurdish insurgents in both Northern and Southern Iraq, killing at least 30-60 000 people during that period.

We know that during his occupation of Kuwait, it is estimated that 1.5 million people were displaced, while the remaining 750 000 endured brutalities, oppression and torture. At least a thousand were killed also in that occupation. Since the Gulf War, Iraqi forces have drained and cleared most of Iraq's Southern Marshlands in an action against the Shiite Muslim Arabs living there. Today most of the 200 000 original inhabitants are displaced and thousands have secretly been executed by Iraqi forces. We also know that Iraq is conducting a systematic 'arabization' campaign of ethnic cleansing, designed to harass and expel ethnic groups such as the Kurds and Turkomen from the government-controlled areas. Non-Iraqi citizens are forced to change their ethnicity, or their identity documents, and adopt Arab names, or else they are deprived of home, property, food rations and are expelled.

Elsewhere Human Rights Watch, together other human rights organizations, have reported the use of rape and sexual assault in a systematic and institutionalized manner for political purposes. Iraqi forces are accused of raping women who are captured during their campaigns. Others detained are routinely and systematically tortured. According to former prisoners, torture techniques include branding, electric shock, beating, burning with hot irons and blowtorches, the breaking of limbs, and the denial of food and water. If an individual survives torture, his or her fate is no better. According to reports received by the UN Special Rapporteur in 1998, hundreds of Kurds and other detainees have been held for nearly two decades in extremely harsh conditions, many of them being used for Iraq's illegal experiments with chemical and biological weapons. With these atrocities, the UN Special Rapporteur stated in 1999 that Iraq remains a country with the highest number of disappearances known to the United Nations. The evidence clearly shows that Saddam Hussein, throughout his decades of dictatorship and defiance, is truly a menace to society.

The threat is real and we have a choice. We can wait and act after countless more deaths, or take action now, on behalf of humanity. The time has come once and for all to put an end to this abuse of power. We must stop the senseless killing, the unnecessary violence, and threats of violence orchestrated by Saddam and his regime. We believe that only a complete change to the current leadership, top to bottom, will resolve the problem. We believe that in order to do this, we must come together in the United Nations and pass an aggressive resolution that will *enforce* the rule of law on behalf of humanity.

It is our responsibility and one that can neither be delegated nor abdicated. To do so would be to acknowledge defeat. Therefore, the United States is prepared to work with the international community to regulate Saddam and his regime, in order to achieve a successful outcome that is so necessary for humanity.

Developing Inter-Cultural Moral Enlightenment for Leaders, Both National and Global

Andrea Bartoli

'Developing inter-cultural moral enlightenment for leaders, both national and global', is an ambitious title and indeed an ambitious task. Let me qualify my position for a moment. I am an anthropologist and I am interested in, and committed to, conflict resolution. The purpose of this article will be to argue about the dynamism of moral standards and the need for new and proper articulation of them. I will take a bold constructive approach, arguing that any gap found between definitions and interpretations of international law and ethics should be welcomed in the first place and then attended to. We are presently facing so many challenges and we need to decide how to respond to them and actually embrace them. Beyond that assertion, we need to promote moral clarity through serious and sustained debate. This timely and relevant conference provides us with an opportunity.

The two themes that the organisers of the conference have suggested are firstly, the widening divergence between the definition of breaches of international law and the interpretation of actual circumstances and events; and secondly, the moral integrity of single-nation, alliance and coalition operations. The underlying assumption is that moral reasoning may provide a positive solution and is actually an indispensable element of it. Indeed, the 'moral high ground' is an essential element of all modern successful operations, a theme which needs elaboration.

The title assigned is curiously positive. I decided not to change it, because 'developing' implies movement and refers to growth, betterment and improvement. It implies that whatever entity, subject, or reality we

---

Dr Andrea Bartoli, trained as an anthropologist, is the founding Director of the Centre of International Conflict Resolution of Columbia University's School of International and Public Affairs. As a member of the Community of St. Egidio, he has worked on conflict resolution in Mozambique, Algeria, Burundi, Kosovo, the Democratic Republic of the Congo, East Timor, Myanmar (Burma) and Northern Iraq.

want to develop needs not to be first destroyed, needs not to be abandoned by the act of 'movement' forward. The term suggests a transformation from within. I think that it is very important, therefore, to acknowledge, that when we address new challenges we need to avoid the temptation to say, 'Well, the old regime doesn't work, we don't need to develop; we need just to abandon the old and then start the new; we need to start afresh'. I believe it is extraordinarily important to acknowledge the existence of a particular attitude in this country. Here, clearly, the rule of law has a long tradition, and while going through very interesting and traumatic challenges, the spirit is never to abandon the hope that actually the rule of law *can* find expression appropriate to a particular event or moment.

Who are the actors, subjects, and protagonists developing law and moral understanding to which we refer in this curiously positive title? The direction that I would like to suggest is that moral development is actually a 'collective experience' which, because it has both a private and public dimension that exists continuously, must be recognized and shared. Such development cannot be just one single episode; it is actually one of those extraordinarily long conversations that goes on for ages.

While it is a dynamic process, I wonder, however, whether it is a linear one. My answer is that we should not be too quick in assuming that we always move in one direction only, that development is necessarily always in a positive direction. Considering the history of collective mass-murder, genocide and widespread violence, it is hard to identify positive linear progression in the century just concluded. At the same time I must admit that I was intrigued by the expression 'moral enlightenment' and its implicitly positive and desirable connotation. For me enlightenment is a cultural term that refers to two very different human experiences. The first is the Hindu and Buddhist spiritual notion of enlightenment, that is 'being enlightened', or 'enlightened beings'; and the second is the very European, secular attempt to understand and foster 'rationality'.

So, is it possible for us to really think about development? I do believe that we can take moral enlightenment partly for granted, beyond the deterministic claim in terms of applicability of ready well-defined norms. We have norms, so our problem seems then just how to apply them. We may go so far as to assume, for example, that Americans would not act in a certain way, because our moral scope is such that it authorizes us to make such a leap. One knows the norm, the regime, the reference points and that certain things do not occur in a particular context. The other side of the argument is to discover how, beyond the easy spiritual claim of others, the moment of collective moral enlightenment is simply unfolding itself. Everyone is carried along together in its changing dynamic. 'I argue that it is the duty of attentive, intelligent, rational, responsible enquiring minds, to never lead us into an easy answer to the question of what is the direction of the enlightenment being sought. We ought to know it. The question still remains of developing the concept of enlightenment and personal dispositions towards it and recognition of achieving complete consensus.

Developing moral enlightenment should be taken seriously, not just the terminology for purposes of knowledge transfer. Sometimes it is too easy to speak about 'moral enlightenment' when the moment arrives with difficult choices to be make. It is no good simply then to describe moral claims in terms of the transfer of knowledge; one norm is like another. It is no good for political leaders to find acknowledged experts on just war to explain the theory of how things should be done properly. The truth is that norms that are unjust and imperfect do not actually represent reality properly and must be reformulated creatively and boldly. At the same time, just and valuable norms must be followed even when they are seen to run counter to someone's immediate interest. Our relationship with norms is that we continuously support and uphold them, not just by having someone else agreeing to relate to them, but living by them personally and directly. There need be no contradiction between norms and moral judgement; one must ally each to other.

The next question is, what are moral relationships in asymmetric war? I would like to start with the fact that many combatants actually claim moral superiority and argue that they are well and absolutely equipped in every moral sense. I think it is important, however, in seeking moral enlightenment to acknowledge the value of 'self-recognition'. One must respect the self-understanding of adversaries and enemies, so that they equally may see themselves as morally very well equipped. In doing so we have to recognize there is a distinction between understanding another's moral position while not necessarily agreeing with and condoning it. This achieved, it is then necessary to move on from the *private* expression of moral claims to recognizable *public* ones, which seems to be the general circumstances that we are all living in today. I would like to add that to understand a moral claim is actually to understand the whole struggle. Failing to recognize that there is morality in someone else's claim prevents us from understanding correctly and properly what the struggle is all about. By proper understanding, we open the door to solutions that would otherwise be simply impossible to conceive and to embrace.

Turning to those actively and directly involved, the reference to a 'moral principle' is frequently used to motivate and sustain combatants themselves. Violent fighting amongst humans has become almost inevitably expressed and elaborated by use of moral terms. However, it is interesting that a trend characterizing liberal democracy seems to be moving in the direction of an international community that accepts many contradictions. The response to the legitimacy of the use of violence does not only come from a counter-claim of the enemy's position; that is to say 'I have the same right that you have to use violence against me in the name of the enmity we share'.

Interestingly enough, one finds a growing sense that the debate is strongest *within* societies. Many would argue that using different moral references within the UK, America and other liberal democracies, societies seem to argue against the use of violence.

Accepting tension and contradiction so that extraordinarily rich moral dissonance can be preserved, is simply a way to give away the debate to the terrorist. Especially in the case of asymmetric war, I would argue that the number of dissenters against action can be significant. Moral ground can be maintained in order to reject a specific strategy. I can be in favour of the war on terrorists, but against keeping people in Guantanamo Bay. I am in favour of the war on terror, but I am against invading Iraq. All these positions are actually mushrooming in liberal democracy and we see the phenomenon of war *and* peace co-existing simultaneously. Motivation can lead us in many directions. Different perspectives emerge in any sector and divide us into 'doves and hawks' and debates of 'yes', 'no' and 'not now, maybe later'.

It is not merely a debate that sets military personnel against civilians, or politicians against civil society. These debates are multi-directional. We have military personnel debating with themselves the wisdom of characterizing action against terrorism in military terms, giving honour and dignity of a war to groups who are simply criminal. There are debates within civil society, fearful of a reduction of civil liberties. There are problems in all sectors of society. The reference to a moral claim by any group, including combatants, needs to be publicly debated, then recognized or rejected.

We know very well that to some or many combatants, war is entirely just and at times even holy. And yet these extraordinary claims are made at the same time as war, as a human collective experience, is actually fading away and becoming irrelevant. After 1945, war has become something very localized and very specific, even if it involves many persons (unfortunately sometimes millions, as in the case of the Congo). Yet war is perceived as distant and particular. So not only do war and peace co-exist within many societies, they co-exist globally. The claims of 'holy' and 'just' wars seem to be necessary ingredients for the world to take any notice.

In pursuing the argument, it is an interesting notion to exist 'at war'. Who is the 'we'? Are all Americans at war? Are the Europeans at war? Who is at war with whom? And who is claiming this war? We heard that Al-Qa'ida wages war against the United States and the West, but who recognized that is indeed 'a war' and not merely criminal activities defined as such? There is something very interesting about defining actions in a certain way, particularly combatants claiming that in considering the war they are maintaining the 'moral high ground'. The war itself, because of the honour involved, the limitations, and the way it is conducted, seizes a moral high ground, expecting success as self-fulfilling prophecy.

Many collective human groups, however, are actually moving away from the idea of just war and holy war. Religious communities are surprisingly outspoken on the idea that no such a thing as a holy war can exist, that there no war or violence can be justified in religious terms. It is not just because of Pope John Paul II's Peace Prayer in 1986. There are many recent pronouncements from churches all over the world. This movement is interesting because it delegitimizes the use of violence as a means of achieving political ends. Conversely, to many combatants war is an inescapable moral duty. You have to fight. It is something that you cannot negotiate; it is part of your own identity; it is part of you own ethos, and the reason you are in uniform.

National and international leaders often may pronounce war-related issues in moral language and terms. Many of the words they use, such as 'evil', refer to moral, even religious categories. I am always perplexed when I hear the attempt to characterize an enemy in absolute evil terms. I think that, as a Christian, such a notion is an impossibility. I think in human beings there is *always* the possibility for reform: this is why civil society is entrusted to guard all of us against evil. Our goal in that sense is to develop morally, by bringing together competing claims, rejecting untruthful ones and embracing those that are constructive.

So how do we develop moral convergence? I think that collective wisdom is formed through sustained and open communication and is crystallized in moments of collective understanding. One of the most fascinating developments in history was immediately after the Second World War when, exhausted by violence, humans finally found a way to represent moral claims in political form and codify them. The Universal Declaration of Human Rights (1948) did not emerge out of a void: it came about out of an understanding of human suffering. The basis for it was an attempt to articulate that human suffering is the common ground that we should refer to when we make a moral judgement. That articulation is certainly not a final one and I believe that the historical movement since 1948 has been the attempt to enrich that framework, to enrich that articulation of moral reference through cataloguing precisely all victimhood and human suffering, through-inter cultural exchanges. Of course moral constructs must be respectful of cultural differences. Describing what is actually happening becomes an attempt to bring together, in tolerance, people representing polarities that would otherwise be unthinkable. In tolerant, sustained communication, a new formulation of shared moral standards may be possible.

I was fascinated by Ambassador Pierre-Richard Prosper's description of the American lead in transforming the United Nations and the international system *[chapter 3]*. I think it is a wonderful development that needs to be welcomed. Also I think that what we need to restrain ourselves from the attempt to control and to hasten processes that actually need time to mature according to their own pace. Transforming moments take place over a long period of time – they do not happen just because we want them to.

One transforming moment was the establishment of the International Criminal Court. It is something that binds together and strengthens states. That having been said, criminals should be prosecuted by nation states before recourse to the International Criminal Court. The Criminal Court intervenes only when national systems do not work properly. Its job is complementary to, and an actual reinforcement of, national laws.

Let me finally introduce a concept on which I am working that I believe may be useful in our debate – the idea of a 'community of interest', and actual communities of those concerned. Those who prompted the debate on the International Criminal Court were not necessarily heads of states but ordinary citizens. I think that we need to be mindful of the possibility that such movements will continue to renew our own understanding of the norms which we are trying to develop and the moral high ground that we want to achieve. My understanding, my wish, is that new institutional legal processes may be identified through and with the UN. I do not think the human family has a better forum. While it is a significant choice for President Bush to speak at the UN of a need for a more forceful enhancement of the rule of law, it is also important to carry along the whole system and not to destroy or abandon it.

Inclusive participation in those debates is the most promising way to develop intercultural moral enlightenment, but it is clear that the strategy of debate presents several challenges. It is slow, cumbersome and unreliable; there is no one controlling it; there is no one single truth. At the same time it is the only chance we have to reduce the possibility of misperception, misconception and misunderstanding. In that sense I would refrain from dividing the world into the enlightened and non-enlightened, and I would also refrain from the temptation of creating a third group who are 'not enlightened yet'.

Intercultural moral enlightenment for national and global leaders is indeed a task for all of us. The use of the Universal Declaration of Human Rights seems to be the most reasonable and promising choice. It is not only a political document; it is a clear expression of a common understanding of morality. If we act sensitively, intelligently and rationally (the responsibility that I was claiming before as an essential component of moral judgement), we may actually end up having a better system. Knowing that, moral standards which are used must be also thoroughly practiced. We should not be using norms and the moral high ground merely as instruments to enforce on others 'enlightenment' that we believe is reasonable. We are seeking something that is true and valuable, even if we can be fallible. The system we want to create shall be a self-correcting system that can indeed continue to develop, as humanity and humankind develops.

Discussion

Military Intervention

Regime change is a declared US aim in resolving the crisis over Iraq. This should be preferably achieved peacefully, but also working with existing opposition groups, so that the democratic process can work to topple Saddam Hussein. This latter possibility, however, has only a slim chance: Saddam Hussein has consistently stifled any sort of democratic development in Iraq. The US is prepared to work in the UN Security Council, to bring strongly to bear existing Security Council Resolutions, but in view of the looming threat of weapons of mass destruction (WMD), the US may not find it possible to wait.

Turning to the difficult distinction between a 'just war' and a 'holy war', in the latter protagonists always claim the higher moral ground. The just war claim put forward by St Thomas Aquinas was in the question 'was it always a sin to wage war?' The answer was 'not if certain conditions are observed' i.e. lawful authority, just cause and right intention. Subsequent thinkers, including Grotius, added the conditions of last resort, reasonable prospect of success, the discrimination between combatants and non-combatants and proportionality between the evils inherent in war on the one hand, and the good achieved or evil averted on the other.

These latter criteria frequently conflict in modern war, and the argument is often put forward that there cannot be such an objective concept as a 'just war'. This argument is either too cynical or simplistic. An overall judgement has to be made to declare a war just or unjust, and inevitably a subjective judgement is always involved.

It is obvious that those involved both in 'just war' and 'holy war' are manifestly using those terms self-referentially. They claim the right to be understood by others in their use of terminology, so as to be justified in taking the actions that they do. In respect of 'holy war', according to Baroness Warnock (a foremost British ethicist), one cannot have morality without there being 'personal choice'. Some cultures are guided by more or less voluntary religions and beliefs, while other cultures are guided by more or less compulsory religions and beliefs. There exists a double dichotomy of 'inclusiveness' and 'exclusiveness', which prevents dialogue and self-correction in accommodating other peoples, of which the worst manifestation is a war between 'cultures'. The bloodiest wars, however, have been waged between Catholics and Protestant Christians, between Shia and Sunni Muslims, for example; and the recent killing of a Jewish Prime Minister by Jewish fundamentalists is another manifestation of the same aspect of human nature. The imperatives of 'inclusiveness' and 'exclusiveness' exist in many religions, but arguably should only be used as a starting point for negotiating an accommodation of other religions and other peoples. Strangely, some religions that once were extraordinarily intolerant have become passionate defenders of plurality and tolerance. There could be a lesson here.

The current provisions of international humanitarian law and other conventions do seem to be firmly based on Judeo-Christian morality. There should, however, be far greater 'ownership' of international law from other legal traditions, for example Islamic law, to promote a 'global ethic' of the best sort of behaviour. Alternatively it could be preferable to insist that, since all legal systems of the World represented through their governments, have already agreed to certain legal and moral principles, they must be complied with under all circumstances, including when the use of armed force is justified. Most religious beliefs actually have an existing universality and consensus: their similarities outweigh their differences.

Even so some religionists, while they can accept what are clearly a set of universal human rights, prefer to claim that those same tenets and truths are such a fundamental part of their beliefs, that they cannot 'give them away' as merely objective goods. To do so would be a denial of their religion. Moral enlightenment and full religious understanding and co-operation, realistically, is very hard to achieve.

There are further distinctions and categories beyond 'just war' and 'holy war': they can be termed 'legal war' and its opposite 'unlawful war'. There is overlap between the categories of 'moral' justification, sometimes based on religious precept, and 'legal' categorization of war. In the early twentieth century, the existing presumption was that war was a means of national policy. This moved on to the belief that war should be 'outlawed' completely (Kellogg-Briand Pact 1928, signed by 65 states) and in 1945 there was established a strong presumption that the abjuration of force was desirable under all circumstances, except if one could point to completely self-evident justification. Self-defence was the original justification under the UN Charter (Article 51). 'Humanitarian intervention' has since then gradually been recognized as a possible lawful justification for the use of force.

These understandings have caused some convergence of legal scholarship with the moral discourse of the churches. Law has the advantage over religions of a 'justificatory system', which all states and governments have accepted through membership of the United Nations. We now seem to be moving further away from the presumption of war being a means merely of national of policy, but that war might be a useful tool of international policy. Moral consensus is recognized by the formation of coalitions of nations willing to act. Threats to international peace and security can thus be interpreted more widely, provided that there is a central institution that determines what can be the 'exceptional' nature and circumstances of the 'threat' to the international community. The difficulty is when one, or a small number of states, claim unilaterally to decide the nature and extent of the threat against the wider international perception and consensus.

Jus in bello

Since at least the time of the Treaty of Westphalia (1648), there has been a strong argument that the application of International Humanitarian Law should be detached from a judgement of whether the war is 'just' or 'not just'. This was challenged in the twentieth century by Soviet doctrine, which insisted that the same rules should not apply to the aggressor as to the victim, the former being the morally culpable party. The more recent case was the self-perception of the North Vietnamese as victims and the captured US pilots as aggressors, therefore beyond the protection of law.

Terminology and the moral inference behind such vocabulary as 'war against evil' and 'war against terrorism' could, by the same token, cause a decline or collapse of humanitarian protection, there being no independent international judge and all parties claiming that 'my cause is just'.

The 'right' use of force consistently maintains and strengthens the distinctions between just war (*jus ad bellum*), conduct in war (*jus in bello*) and International Humanitarian Law. You can indeed lose the 'just war' claim if you are in breach of International Humanitarian Law, since your 'just cause' can diminish rapidly. Labelling people as 'unlawful combatants' is also something that should be handled with very great caution, as is confining persons to prison on an island, such as Cuba, beyond the reach of law.

Behaviour of all parties to intervention, conflict resolution and peacekeeping missions needs, to attain, and continue to meet, high moral standards at all times. In regard to the unacceptable behaviour of some Afghan 'warlords' holding former Taliban captives, the international peacekeeping coalition has had to take action. Investigation of the reported circumstances of a thousand or more people confined in trucks and containers in which many suffered and died, has to be conducted, including if needs be exhumation of bodies from graves and forensic evidence gathering. Accountability must be subsequently determined, and it is important that the Afghan authorities play a fundamental role in the process as part of their national democratic development.

In respect of the jurisdiction of the International Criminal Court, the US wishes that national institutions can be built or rebuilt internally. That will be better for their own democratic development. Nations should never absolve themselves of all responsibility, because justicial procedures are too difficult to apply. Likewise, the US will continue to impress on both Israel and the Palestinian authorities to fulfil all their international obligations and reach a lasting settlement of their dispute.

Other moral arguments often arise, such as whether special humanitarian rules should be developed for separate regions, for instance in Africa and the Middle East. This would be a great danger: most conflicts take place on the border between cultures and civilizations. One cannot emphasize enough that most nations of the world have already taken part in all the negotiations drawing up International Humanitarian Law, and should continue to hold those laws universally and as objectively derived. Furthermore nations should beware of loose application of the concept and terminology of 'war'.

How state sovereignty is defined, however, continues to be debated, particularly when there is a 'just cause' put forward for secession of constituent parts of an existing nation-state. There remains a tension between free will and self-determination on the one hand, and on the other, long-held constitutional agreements and geopolitical status. The notion of 'self-determination' has given encouragement to many secessionary movements to attempt to detach their territory by force, such as during the Biafran War (1968-70), or by other means, such as achieved peacefully in Bangladesh (1972). In such conflicts the 'international system' normally seems to favour the state 'winning'. While the case of Chechnya remains, there have nevertheless been a dozen recent cases in which countries have reconstructed themselves reasonably satisfactorily, to re-accommodate would–be secessionists. We have moved on from the narrow decolonization notion of 'self-determination'.

Jus ad bellum

On the subject of inter-state conflict, the distinctions between

- Preventative war,
- Pre-emptive strike, and
- Anticipatory self-defence,

must be clearly understood. A preventative war, such as the US is proposing against Iraq, is so called when military action is taken before the danger is immediately manifest. A pre-emptive strike is much more immediate, when a would-be aggressor is ready and just waiting for a final decision to launch an attack. Anticipatory self-defence is the only one which has, at least until recently, been legal, that is when a chain of events has already been set in motion. The landing of an imminent attack on your territory by overwhelming means is expected, with no instant choice of other means of defence left open to you. 'Imminence' is demonstrated for instance, by Saddam Hussein filling his missiles with VX gas, adding rocket fuel, having set in motion the decision that these weapons will be employed. The principle here is that you do not have to wait until they land on your territory, before you strike against those missiles on their launching pads. Instant, overwhelming threat, with 'no moment of deliberation', is the test.

Some lawyers will argue that there should be more flexibility of definition between the three categories. History reveals that the attack by Israel on (French-built) nuclear reactors in Iraq (May 1981) was declared unlawful by the UN Security Council. That decision was supported by the US government, and compensation ordered (but never paid). Perhaps we are witnessing a return to the practicalities of the period before 1928 (when the Kellogg-Briand Pact was signed), when force had a different meaning and currency.

Finally, since the use of force is defined as organized violence, the question of moral and legal justification of the acts of leaders and followers, war-lords and tribesman, has to be considered. Personal and group loyalties to such politico-religious groups as the Taliban further confuses the question. Arguably, there is no real escape from personal moral responsibility – personal identity and identification with a group notwithstanding. If the group switches allegiance and acts cooperatively with others, in for instance moving away from authoritarianism toward democracy, personal loyalty can turn out to be a positive factor. Despite the pessimism surrounding the current world crises, new factors and new ways are being sought and found in a spirit of optimism, which can overcome some of the legal and moral dilemmas which beset international affairs.

Chapter 4

Military Interventions

The Ethics of Counter-terrorism

Alistair Irwin

I shall start by quoting from a chapter about asymmetric warfare that I contributed to a book entitled *'Military Power'* (edited by Professor Brian Holden Reid). I wrote, referring to terrorists and their like as minimalists:

> For the minimalist there are no rules, no uniforms, no front line, no inhibitions or limitations, no territory to defend. So the minimalist can choose where and when to strike; he can appear and disappear, cloaking himself in the darkness of the underworld. For those that oppose him, the difficulties are intense. These are not two boxers facing each other in the dark (you will recall Liddell Hart's concept of the Man in the Dark), but rather two boxers one of whom is invisible. How can he be found if he cannot be seen? How can he be attacked if he cannot be found? The minimalist has all the advantages.[1]

Although I was concentrating specifically on the operational aspects of terrorism and counter terrorism, I want to pick up on those phrases 'no rules', and 'no inhibitions or limitations'. It seems to be the case that terrorists have the advantage of us in terms of the law and morality, just as much as they do operationally.

If we are discussing asymmetry, then we might very well describe the phenomenon of this advantage as *asymmetric morality*. Or, more precisely, asymmetric morality and legality as it applies to that part of asymmetric warfare, which encompasses terrorism.

But first I must introduce a very important disclaimer. I have had a very wide and very long experience of the military involvement in Northern Ireland, experience that is capped in every possible sense by my previous appointment as GOC. Obviously my experience has heavily influ-

---

Lieutenant-General Sir Alistair Irwin is Adjutant General and formerly was General Officer Commanding Northern Ireland, where he has served operationally in every level of appointment. He was commissioned into and later commanded The Black Watch (Royal Highland regiment) and his appointments included Directing Staff at the Army Staff College, Director Land warfare, Commandant RMCS and Military Secretary.

enced the way in which I think about these sort of things but I would like it to be clear that, although I shall refer to Ireland once or twice, the remarks that follow are not intended to be interpreted as implicit or explicit commentaries on current or past military actions or operational methods in the Province. My very clear intent is to discuss in generalities and specifically from the point of view of a current practitioner.

What, if anything, can be done about moral asymmetry and the conundrum that it presents? I will start with the terrorist. It is obviously the case that he has no inhibitions about breaking the law, even (perhaps especially) the law of democratic liberal states – it is not possible otherwise to be a terrorist. So there is nothing remarkable in that. But what *is* remarkable is that so many commentators, and public opinion, do not seem to be repelled by that.

There is of course revulsion at the outcome of specific acts that lead to death or destruction. But the generality of breaking the law or offending against accepted moral codes, inherently and perpetually, does not seem to score such a black mark as to undermine fatally either the ability of the terrorist to operate, or the standing of his political negotiators. And, of course, the practical consequence is that the terrorist can decide to do literally anything that he likes absolutely uninhibited by the knowledge that it is against the law or the Ten Commandments. There are no principled obstacles in the way of his freedom of action except those that he imposes on himself for pragmatic reasons.

This lack of inhibition gives him another supreme trump card. He can lie, he can lay any false accusations and he can run a propaganda campaign that has the potential to undermine his opponents just as much as if he used any form of physical violence. In many ways I happen to think that this is the most powerful weapon that a terrorist has to his hand. It is one that has been exploited with ruthless efficiency and effect by the IRA. And, funnily enough, it is this that can aggravate a government far more than any death or destruction because it is so utterly corrosive and wholly devoid of any basis for sympathy for those that are attacked.

A terrorist attack that maims or kills a member of the security forces may be thought to be serving the terrorist's purposes but the effect is dissipated by the sympathy that is extended towards the victim. Accuse the same soldier or policeman of brutality or political bias and you lay the foundation for the alienation of the population from the forces of law and order, without the disadvantage of inspiring sympathy for the accused. Lying is indeed a powerful weapon particularly (but not necessarily) if, as in all the best propaganda, the lie has some small grain of truth in it.

In the same way the terrorist, being wholly unabashed about the prospect of lying, can turn the tables by inverting his own immorality to make it look as though he is walking with the angels. Thus it was possible recently for Republicans to proclaim without a blush that:

> If it were not for the IRA there would be no peace process.

And nor, they conspicuously fail to add, would there ever have been the need for one in the first place. And all the while, thugs prowl about handing out what they disgracefully term 'community justice' to those that have offended them. This is not the sort of justice that leads to fines or community service or even judicial sentences to terms of imprisonment, but to shots in the elbows, the knees and the buttocks. Or to savage beatings. Or to murder. And these actions are carried out in the name of law and order. The terrorist has an infinite capacity to flout the law, to break it and to dishonour it by carrying out reprehensible actions in the name of it.

And what about those who operate against the terrorist? My remarks are going to be predicated on the assumption that it is the counter-terrorism practised by democracies that interests us. Democracies, of course, insist on upholding the law as a fundamental principle. Not all regimes give themselves this restriction. Counter-terrorism as practised by dictatorships and police states is an altogether different matter. It is perfectly possible, as a matter of policy, to take actions against terrorists that trample all over the basic principles of law and human rights.

I shall return, by implication, to this entirely counter-productive form of counter-terrorism, while noting the interesting issues that arise, if and when, democracies with one set of values find themselves in coalition with allies with other views.

So, democracies are expected to behave in a way that is entirely consistent with the law. Many describe it as operating with one arm tied behind the back because, so it is argued, the terrorist can only be beaten by joining him in the darkness of the underworld and copying his illegal methods.

But in those societies in which the rule of law is treasured, any breaking of the law by counter-terrorist forces will be unsympathetically exposed and condemned. The opprobrium that attaches to national institutions that act illegally is infinitely greater than anything that attaches to the terrorists themselves.

By the same token, there is little or no possibility of lying and getting away with it. Even factual inaccuracies in reporting the circumstances of an incident will be put down to some sort of conspiracy, when it is normally nothing more than the product of the usual sort of confusion and chaos that occurs in the wake of a shooting or whatever. The nonsense that is put out by the terrorist may or not be believed, but if it is discovered to be untrue no one thinks anything of it – it is what is expected. An untrue statement by those defending a democracy is castigated – because democracies are expected to tell the truth.

I shall return to this point but for now I am going to try to explain why it so important that, whatever the provocation, it is vital to those who seek to overcome terrorists that they stay firmly on the right side of the law. On the right side of what is right and wrong. I think that there are at least four reasons.

The first is a matter of common humanity. What merit is there in fighting one form of immorality with another; why should anyone support you in doing so? No one, winner or loser, will survive unscathed as a moral being if he deliberately flouts the law, especially if such activity leads to someone's death. And worse, no member of the organization, or even nation, to which that person belongs, can possibly dismiss it all later as having been of no significance. In one way or another it will come back to bite you. I do not say that every single one of us will be perpetually smitten by a guilty conscience – regrettably there are many in all walks of life who appear to be wholly unaffected by the ghastly things that they, or the organizations to which they belong, have done to people in their past.

But remorse is no doubt an uncomfortable companion as one passes through life and it can creep up without warning and once there never goes away. One thinks of the anguish experienced by many French officers and men who came to regret the part they had played in the torturing of Algerian suspects particularly during the Battle of Algiers. Alistair Horne tells us that the Anglo-American journalist with the improbable name of Edward Behr recorded his opinion that:

> Without torture the FLN's terrorist network would never have been overcome… The Battle of Algiers could not have been won by General Massu without the use of torture.[2]

But Albert Camus balances this by observing:

> Torture has perhaps saved some at the expense of honour, by uncovering thirty bombs, but at the same time it has created fifty new terrorists who, operating in some other way and in another place, would cause the death of even more innocent people. It is better to suffer certain injustices than to commit them.

The dilemma is nicely revealed in the episode in which a terrorist was caught red-handed laying one of two bombs that he was known to have. Despite his obvious guilt he refused to say where the other bomb was placed. The official in charge was encouraged to order the torture of the prisoner to extract the required information. The official had been a prisoner of the Germans in Dachau and had himself been tortured there. He takes up the tale like this:

> But I refused to have him tortured. I trembled the whole afternoon. Finally the bomb did not go off. Thank God I was right. Because if you once get into the torture business, you're lost..... Understand this, fear was the basis of it all. All our so-called civilisation is covered with a varnish. Scratch it, and underneath you find fear. The French, even the Germans, are not torturers by nature. But when you see the throats of your copains slit, then the varnish disappears.[3]

In my view the job of the counter terrorist is to do what he can to preserve that coat of varnish in a good state of repair.

The second reason is a matter of practicality, what one might call the law of unintended long-term consequences. Whether we are talking of warfighting or of counter terrorism we can all doubtless call quickly to mind the counter-productive effects of engaging in illegal acts, especially those that involve excessive violence. No doubt you will have your own examples of where barbarism has been allowed to intrude into the already gruesome business of fighting. I am reminded of the great Liberal leader Henry Campbell Bannerman's question in the House of Commons at the time of the Boer War:

> When is war not a war – when it is carried out by methods of barbarism in South Africa.[4]

Operating outside the law and the moral code may very possibly solve an immediate tactical or even operational problem. But it will surely encourage a tougher resistance, a greater resolve to dish out the same medicine in the opposite direction. Read of the grim activities of the Red Army 2nd echelon forces moving into Berlin behind the assault troops and recognize the fruit of the efforts of the German *Einsatzgruppen* and *Sonderkommando* in the rear areas of the Eastern Front in the glory days before defeat. Consider the brutal retaliations after resistance, partisan and guerrilla attacks round the world and through the ages and see how the tendency is for the resistance to strengthen.

There is nothing long-term to be gained by inspiring the fear, the hatred and the contempt of the population. I might add that security force *mistakes* that lead to illegal or immoral actions resulting in death and destruction have as much negative impact as if those same actions were deliberately wilful.

In this context we might invoke the memory of a young Stern Gang member in Palestine. In May 1947 Alexander Rubowitz disappeared, believed murdered by a small group of men led by a much-decorated SAS officer called Roy Farran. This outfit was modelled on the Special Night Squads that had been established in the same region before the War, strangely enough on the suggestion of Air Commodore 'Bomber' Harris and which included Orde Wingate in their number. Farran apparently believed that he had been given a free hand to act against terrorists. Of course, he had not been and he was tried by court martial for the murder of Rubowitz.

Although he was acquitted, the public perception of what had been going on could be said to have inspired an unforeseen and wholly negative chain reaction. Possibly in retaliation for Rubowitz's murder, two British NCOs were kidnapped and later hanged. Their bodies were strung up in a eucalyptus tree and booby-trapped. The officer who came to cut them down was severely injured. Violent reprisals by troops and police in Tel Aviv culminated in the machine-gunning of Jewish shops and cafés by police armoured cars. Five people were killed. And what purpose was served other than to strengthen support for those who were (to borrow the full title of the Stern Gang) 'fighting for the freedom of Israel'? What was remembered? The murder of Rubowitz and the security force violence in Tel Aviv. The lynching of the NCOs and the maiming of the officer were lost in the propaganda noise.

We might also remember the imposition in 1921 of martial law in the four southwestern counties of Ireland, where General Strickland let it be known that: 'An attitude of neutrality is inconsistent with loyalty.'

Official punishments were instigated as a form of legal reprisal. They included the destruction of any house from which shots were fired at the security forces or from which the preparations for an IRA ambush could have been seen and should have been reported to the authorities. It is perhaps not surprising that this part of Ireland was always one of the staunchest areas of republican sympathy.

So, the counter-terrorist must be sure that today's solution is not the seed of tomorrow's insoluble problem.

The third reason that we must stick to the right side of the law is that we now operate in a contemporary environment in which there is an army of organizations and bodies prowling the touchline watching for every infringement of the rules. Broadcast and print journalists, human rights bodies, lawyers seeking compensation for their clients and politicians with a mission are amongst those who are constantly on the alert for the false move.

I once made a study of the British experience of what we at one time called counter-revolutionary warfare. On the whole we had a pretty successful record in the sense that insurrections were extinguished. But some of the methods used were by our modern standards extraordinarily heavy-handed and would have given ample cause for the touchline spectators to give tongue to their complaints.

I think, for example, of the 2 300 Moplah rebels killed on the Malabar Coast in 1921 during a counter-insurgency campaign that lasted only a few months, among them 70 Moplahs locked up in a train. In the extreme heat, they all suffocated and died in an uncomfortable reverse echo of the Black Hole of Calcutta. There is no doubt that if the observers to whom I have referred had existed 80 years ago the Moplah rebels would either have been treated differently or someone's head would certainly have rolled, even though the GOC Madras was at the time:

> Satisfied that punishment had fallen on the guilty and that no lesser chastisement would have sufficed to bring the fanatical and misguided community to their senses.

Yet, General Dyer's head rolled after the well-known shooting in the Jallianwalla Bagh in Amritsar two years before the Moplah uprising; reminding us that consideration for human rights is by no means a product of the late twentieth century.

Nevertheless, in those days it was a very rudimentary kind of consideration, now it is very well defined. The counter-terrorist cannot turn a blind eye to the existence of all those people and organizations who see it as their business to keep everyone else on the straight and narrow. One could wish however that they carried out their necessary and very often invaluable duties more even-handedly and with a more obviously understanding disposition. An apologist for General Dyer, his contemporary biographer Ian Colvin, made this interesting observation quoting the then Adjutant General in India, Sir Havelock Hudson:

> No more distasteful or responsible duty falls to the lot of the soldier than that which he is sometimes required to discharge in aid of the civil power. If his measures are too mild, he fails in his duty. If they are deemed to be excessive, he is liable to be attacked as a cold-blooded murderer. His position is one demanding the highest degree of sympathy from all reasonable and right-mind-

> ed citizens. He is frequently called upon to act on the spur of the moment in grave situations in which he intervenes, because all the other resources of civilisation have failed. His actions are liable to be judged by *ex post facto* standards, and by persons who are in complete ignorance of the realities he had to face. His good faith is liable to be impugned by the very persons connected with the organisation of the disorders which his action has foiled. There are those who will admit that a measure of force may be necessary, but who cannot agree with the extent of the force employed. How can they be in a better position to judge of that than the officer on the spot?

Quite so. Today's counter-terrorist will always find himself being judged by those *ex post facto* standards. So he must indeed be scrupulous in his actions.

The fourth reason for sticking to the law follows neatly on, for it is a matter of history. So long as we can go to our graves with a clear conscience I suppose it does not matter greatly to us how posterity may or may not judge our actions. But it does matter very much to those that follow us. I know that I derive much of my pride in being in the British Army from the great deeds of the Army in the past. That pride is tempered by the knowledge that not everything went quite so well but I am very grateful that the good things so obviously outweigh the bad. I doubt if I would have much pride if the Army's history were one of undiluted failure and immorality.

So each succeeding generation has the duty to lay down, as best it can, a new chapter of achievements in which people can be proud in the future. Of course, I doubt, and so do you, that decisions are made on this basis alone but one hopes that this will be the natural consequence of following the imperative of the other three reasons.

So, is there ever an occasion when a democracy should deliberately remove that French official's 'varnish on civilization'? I once asked that question of an eminent QC specialising in human rights. How is it possible, I asked, for a democracy to defend itself without occasionally or usually resorting to torture, summary arrest and detention without trial, assassination and so on? After all, I suggested, we know who these people are and see them on a daily basis – we just do not enough evidence to put them before a court of law. He replied by asking me another set of questions. Do the papers get delivered? Can you safely get to hospital? Do the trains run? Can your children go to school? If the answer is yes there is no reason for the varnish to slip. Only when the whole structure of society is collapsing and anarchy is imminent should democracies allow themselves to take desperate measures and then only through legislation.

So, except in dire *extremis* those fighting terrorism are bound to be constrained in what they do. Not so their opponents. They can advance their cause by murdering; we cannot. They can advance their cause by spinning a vast web of lies and deceit; we cannot. They are aided in this by an audience that often seems to be either gullible or inherently prejudiced, apparently all too ready to believe the worst of the counter-terrorist, perversely giving at least as much weight to the word of those habitually operating outside the law, as to the word of those who habitually operate inside it.

What is the answer to the conundrum thus posed? The military man, the negotiator, the politician, indeed anyone with a rival, having identified the opposition's advantage will obviously seek to reduce or eliminate that advantage.

I think that in the case of asymmetric morality we cannot just sit back and take the blows, merely expecting or hoping that right will eventually prevail – that is asking a little much of even the most even-tempered of nations. If we cannot match the terrorist lie for lie and crime for crime, we can at least minimize his advantage and give a fair wind to that expectation and hope by taking three simply stated actions.

The first concerns training. It strikes me that in all my time in the Army no one has ever once talked in the terms that I just have in the context of preparing troops, and especially their commanders, to deal with this particular issue. Forewarned is forearmed and to recognize the importance of asymmetric morality in the terrorist armoury is to win half the battle.

The second is ensuring that when the law is broken (as it is bound to be from time to time either by mistake, or wilfully by those bad apples that can be found in any large organization) immediate remedial action is taken. It has to be seen to be scrupulously and swiftly applied, allowing no opportunity for the terrorist and his sympathizer to exploit any shortcomings. This involves admitting the action, apologising and compensating for it, and punishing the guilty party. Swift and exemplary public action, preferably beating the propagandists to the draw, will pay enormous dividends for it will allow the counter-terrorist to claim and secure the high moral ground no matter what assaults are made on it. It will of course lend greater credibility to the denials of those things of which they stand accused but which they have in fact not done.

And gradually by degrees this sort of open, honest, even humble, way of proceeding will be favourably compared with the dissembling, the cheating and the hypocrisy of the opposition. And if it is done really well it may even be that in time the terrorist's advantage derived from asymmetric morality will become a disadvantage. But, this will only work if it is followed as a strategy from the very outset. Once the moral high ground is lost it is almost impossible to regain.

The third action is about having a really good counter-terrorist strategy involving all the elements of government that have a part to play. The Malayan example is instructive here, I think. The strategy must then be supported by highly appropriate police and, if necessary, military action. And, crucially in the context of my subject there must be a centrally coordinated information strategy which recognizes the importance of the terrorists' propaganda machinery and which deliberately sets out to minimize the value that the terrorist derives from it.

I said these three things are simply stated but they are not easy to put into effect. The information strategy is perhaps the most difficult aspect of the whole lot but that is no excuse for not having a plan. If any of this were easy we might not have quite the difficulties that we all face in dealing with a scourge that is an outrage to all that is good in humanity. And, even if we allow ourselves to believe that the terrorist will always have the advantage over us, I am as certain as I can be that Albert Camus was right when he said:

> It is better to suffer certain injustices than to commit them.

NOTES

1 Brian Holden Reid (ed) *Military Power: Land Warfare in Theory and Practice* (London, Frank Cass, 1997).

2 Alistair Horne, *A Savage War of Peace* (London, Papermac, 1991), p. 205.

3 Alistair Horne, *A Savage War of Peace* (London, Papermac, 1991) p. 204.

4 See e.g Thomas Pakenham, *The Boer War*, (London, Weidenfeld and Nicolson, 1982), chapter 39.

Educating the Stoic Warrior

Nancy Sherman

In a remarkably prescient moment, James B. Stockdale, then a senior Navy pilot shot down over Vietnam, muttered to himself as he parachuted into enemy hands, 'Five years down there, at least. I'm leaving behind the world of technology and entering the world of Epictetus.'[1] Epictetus' famous handbook the *Enchiridion* was Stockdale's bedtime reading in the many carrier wardrooms he occupied as he cruised the waters off Vietnam in the mid-1960s. Stoic philosophy resonated with Stockdale's temperament and profession, and he committed much of Epictetus' pithy remarks to memory. Little did he know on that 'shoot down day' of 9 September 1965 that Stoic tonics would hold the key to his survival for six years of prisoner-of-war (POW) life. They would also form the backbone of his leadership style as the senior officer in the POW chain of command.

It does not take too great a stretch of the imagination to think of a POW survivor as a kind of Stoic sage. For the challenge the POW lives with is just the Stoics' challenge: to find dignity when stripped of nearly all nourishments of the body and soul. Stoicism is a philosophy of defence, a philosophy of 'sucking it up'. On a strict reading, it minimizes vulnerability by denying the intrinsic goodness of things that lie outside one's control. In many ways, boot camp is a green soldier's early lesson in Stoicism.

Indeed, in general, it is easy to think of military men and women as 'stoics.' The very term has come to mean in our vernacular 'controlled,' disciplined,' 'not easily agitated or disturbed.' Military officers tend to cultivate these character traits. In a vivid way, they live out the consolations

Professor Nancy Sherman formerly of Harvard, Yale and Johns Hopkins universities, is Professor of Philosophy at Georgetown University, and served as inaugural holder of the Distinguished Chair in Ethics at the US Naval Academy from 1997 to 1999. She has written extensively on military ethics and is working on the forthcoming book *The Stoic Warrior* for Oxford University Press.

of Stoic practical philosophy. In this paper I want to explore certain aspects of military moral education by returning to ancient Stoic teachings.

In 1997 I was appointed the inaugural Distinguished Chair in Ethics at the Naval Academy. I was 'brought aboard' this naval establishment to teach what American and European universities had been teaching for the better part of a century. But at the Naval Academy, even an introduction to ethics had passed the students by. Leadership courses were standard, with a mix of management and motivational psychology, yet the far more ancient subject of ethics was somehow viewed as newfangled, a possibly heretical academic course that would dare to teach what ought to be bred in the bones. I was to teach ethics for the military. That was contractual. What was not prearranged was what the military would teach me. They would allow me entrance into a world that for many of my generation had been cut off by Vietnam and had remained largely impregnable ever since. And they would offer something of a living example of the doctrines of Stoicism I had studied only before as texts.

The allure of Stoicism became explicit at a certain point in the semester each term. The course I taught covered topical themes on honesty, liberty, virtue, and just war interwoven with the writings of historical figures, such as Aristotle and Aquinas, John Stuart Mill and Kant, and Epictetus as a representative Stoic. It was when we arrived at Epictetus that many felt they had come home. What resonated with them was what resonated with Jim Stockdale as he read Epictetus each night.

> There are things which are within our power, and there are things which are beyond our power. Within our power are opinion, aim, desire, aversion, and in one word, whatever affairs are our own. Beyond our power are body, property, reputation, office, and in one word, whatever are not properly our own affairs.
>
> ... Remember, then, that if you attribute freedom to things by nature dependent and take what belongs to others for your own, you will be hindered, you will lament, you will be disturbed, your will find fault both with gods and men...If it concerns anything beyond our power, be prepared to say that it is nothing to you.[2]

Epictetus is right to think that our opinions, desires, and emotions are in our power, not in the radical sense that we can produce them, instantly, at will, but in the sense that we can do things, indirectly, to shape them. And he is right to think, with the Stoics in general, that our opinions about self and others influence our desires and emotions. In contrast, we have far less control over other sorts of goods. A Marine may be killed in friendly fire that he had no way of avoiding, a sailor may be deserving of decoration and promotion but be overlooked because of gender prejudice that she alone cannot change, stocks may take a nose dive however prudent one's investments. A Stoic like Epictetus reminds us of the line that divides what is and what is not within our control. He reminds us that we will be miserable if our happiness itself depends too heavily upon things over which we have little dominion. The Stoic recommendation is not complacency or a retreat to a narrow circle of safety. We are to continue to meet challenges and take risks, and stretch the limits of our mastery. We are to continue to strive to the best of our efforts to achieve our ends, but we must learn greater strength in the face of what we simply cannot change.

Who are the Stoics from whom the military takes implicit guidance? Epictetus has been mentioned, but we need to put his writings in historical context. Roughly speaking, the ancient Stoics span the period from 300 BC to AD 200. They are part of the broad Hellenistic movement of philosophy that follows upon Aristotle and includes, in addition to Stoicism, ancient Skepticism and Epicureanism. The early Greek Stoics, known as the old Stoa (taking their name from the stoa, or painted colonnade near the central piazza of Athens where disciples paced back and forth) were interested in systematic philosophical thought that joined ethics together with studies in physics and logic. The works of the founders of the school, such as Zeno, Cleanthes, and Chrysippus, survive only in fragments quoted by later writers. Indeed, much of what we know about Stoicism comes through Roman redactors like Cicero, Seneca, Epictetus, and Marcus Aurelius. These Roman redactors, some writing in Greek, like Epictetus and Marcus Aurelius, others writing in Latin, like Seneca and Cicero, viewed themselves as public philosophers at the centre of public life.

Cicero (106-43BC), the well-known Roman political orator, consul, and ally to Pompey, turned to specifically philosophical writing at the end of his political career after Caesar's assassination, (which Cicero viewed as a tyrannicide), and while in hiding from his own future assassins, Antony and the other triumvirs. Though himself not a Stoic (rather he identified as a member of the New Academy or school of Skepticism), he wrote extensively on Stoic views and his work, especially *On Ends* and *On Duties*, remained highly influential throughout the Renaissance and Enlightenment as statements of Stoic positions. Seneca, writing in the mid-first century AD, was the tutor and political advisor of the young emperor Nero. Among other things, he wrote voluminously on the passions, and how anger, hatred, and envy, if not understood and properly reined in, can ruin a ruler and bring down a commonwealth. He also wrote about attachment and fortune, and how we can learn to become less vulnerable to their vicissitudes. Epictetus, a Greek slave turned philosopher who also wrote in the time of Nero's reign, greatly influenced Marcus Aurelius. Epictetus' aphoristic writings, summarized in a popular handbook, teach about the power of our minds and imagination to find a measure of mastery and fulfilment even in enslavement.

Marcus Aurelius, a Roman emperor and warrior, wrote his famous *Meditations* in AD 172 in the fleeting moments of quiet he was able to snatch during the German campaigns. In contrast to Seneca's writings, which are often addressed to others, Marcus's meditations are exhortations to himself, about his status as a 'citizen of the world' and the community of humanity and god linked through reason and law with nature. He warns how one can be lured away from reason by the attractions of 'place or wealth or pleasurable indulgence,' and how a zeal for glory can pervert happiness. A repeated theme is that we live in a Heraclitean world of flux. To find happiness, we cannot hold on too tight to what is transient and beyond our control.

The Stoics teach self-sufficiency and the importance of detaching ourselves from dependence on worldly goods that make us vulnerable. In a similar fashion, they advocate a detachment from sticky emotions that mark our investments in things beyond our control. The soldier preparing for battle heeds that advice in a manner of speaking. A Navy flier, with whom I taught at the Academy, once told me that before he went on a mission, he would take control of his emotions by uttering the mantra, 'compartmentalize, compartmentalize, compartmentalize'. The trick, of course, is to know when to compartmentalize and when not to. Mission preparedness seems to require it. But full Stoic detachment from the kind of emotions that record connection as well as loss can be too high a price to pay, even for the warrior. In particular, the capacity to grieve, to mourn one's dead, is crucial for warrior survival.

Consider Coriolanus, the legendary warrior in the fifth century BC who turns against his native city for banishing him. He is portrayed by Shakespeare as the paragon Stoic warrior. Physically strong and detached, more at home in the battlefield than with his wife and son, he is the military man *par excellence*. Fearless, he sheds few tears, and yet the play's turning point comes when Coriolanus remembers how to weep. 'It is no little thing,' he concedes, 'to make mine eyes to sweat compassion.' (*Coriolanus*, Act V scene iii) It is Coriolanus' mother, Volumnia, who reawakens his soul. Her entreaties persuade him to quit his siege of Rome and to restore peace. In weeping, Coriolanus finds human dignity.

Coriolanus may be a loner, a mama's boy at heart, touched only by a mother's tears. But for most soldiers, combat itself nurtures a camaraderie and attachment akin to the family relationships of childhood. The friendship of Achilles and Patroclus, central to the *Iliad*, symbolizes brothers-in-arms for all time. We cannot begin to understand Achilles' near suicidal mourning for Patroclus without appreciating the sheer intensity of that bond. Moreover, we're misled if we think, as many readers have, that a friendship so passionate must be sexual, that only warrior/ lovers could grieve as Achilles does for Patroclus.[3] Whether sexual partners or not, Achilles's grief for Patroclus could not be greater. The *Iliad*, like much of Greek culture, celebrates *philia*, the bond of friendship, with all its passion and shared journeys. It recognizes the dignity of grief that comes when death or separation breaks the bond.

In contemporary war, too, where soldiers put themselves at risk to defend each other, where Marines risk the living to save the dead or those with little breath left, the camaraderie of brothers and sisters-in-arms underwrites the sacrifices. But contemporary combat soldiers don't always have time to grieve. Indeed, in missions where combat rarely stops, where pilots catapult from carriers only seconds after learning that the sorties before them will never return, where vets come home in one's and two's aboard commercial airlines (as they did from Vietnam) and not en masse with their cohorts (as my father did from the Second World War aboard the converted RMS *Queen Mary*), there is little time or place to sweat tears of compassion. And yet deferring grief has devastating psychological costs.

The issues are raised penetratingly by Jonathan Shay, in *Achilles in Vietnam* (1994). As a Vietnam veterans' psychiatrist, he urges that communal grief work must again take place, as it did in the ancient world of the *Iliad*, if we are to help soldiers avoid the living death of post combat trauma. As many of his patients say, 'I died in Vietnam.' Like Achilles at the death of Patroclus, they view themselves as already dead and deadened by losing a close friend, 'another self,' as Aristotle would say.

Of course, the orthodox Stoic might say loss is not real loss if it falls outside what we can control through our own effort and virtue. We would do better to change our habits of attachment than to pamper those whose false attachments create their losses. But we can learn from Stoicism without embracing its strict letter. We can learn that in the midst of our grieving, we still have a home in the world, connected to others whose fellowship and empathy supports us, that we have inner resources that allow us to stand again after we have fallen. This is the human side of Stoicism that can toughen us without robbing us of our humanity.

I am reminded here of a stony-faced Marine colonel, who confided in me one evening that his most wrenching experience in war came not on the battlefield but in leaving behind his first born, a one and a half year-old boy. Going down to the plane, as he began his unaccompanied mission, his guts began to seize up on him. 'I literally became sick to my stomach and vomited the whole way. I was violently ill the whole flight.'

Another colleague told me that flying planes was easy. He said he was even amazed that he was paid to do what he loved. What was agony was leaving his wife and child behind. Nothing made that easier. Nothing could. These are tough warriors, Stoic warriors, but they are made of human stuff. They sweat tears of compassion. They heave their guts out when they leave their loved ones.

Other traditions before and after Stoicism present from the start a philosophy with softer, human lines. So Aristotle emphasizes throughout his ethical and political writings that the attachments of friendship are an irreducible part of a good life. To lose a beloved friend is to lose part of what counts for happiness. One's own goodness cannot make up the difference. One necessarily relies on the goodness of others to complete one's own goodness. Similarly, Judeo-Christian traditions emphasize love and compassion and the healing power of each. In Exodus 15.26, God is portrayed as fearful and awesome, but also the first time in the bibical narrative as a healer, ready to protect the Israelites against disease and ready to provide them with water and bread in their 40 days and 40 nights trekking through the wilderness.

The Stoics may struggle to capture the full palette of emotional attachment, but they do profoundly recognize our cosmopolitan status in the world. And they stress, in a way significant for military education, the respect and empathy required of citizens of the world. In *On Anger*, Seneca reminds his interlocutor, Novatus, that he is a citizen not just of his country but of that 'greater city' of his, that universal commonwealth of the cosmos.[4] Each of us is a 'world citizen,' the Stoics emphasize, following Diogenes the Cynic's notion of the human as a *kosmpolitês*, literally, 'cosmic, universal citizen.'[5] We are each parts of an extended commonwealth and risk our individual integrity, our wholeness, when we sever ourselves from the fellowship of that community. Marcus Aurelius makes the point graphically in terms of a much-used Stoic metaphor of the organic body:

> If you have ever seen a dismembered hand or foot or head cut off, lying somewhere apart from the rest of the trunk, you have an image of what a man makes of himself...when he...cuts himself off and does some unneighbourly act...For you came into the world as a part and you have cut yourself off.[6]

Thus, on the Stoic view, it is as if we mutilate ourselves when we cut ourselves off from the global community. The notion of extended world citizenship became relevant to my Navy students as they prepared to risk their lives in foreign corners of the world and serve in multi-national coalitions. Many students actively wrestled with what they saw as competing views of allegiance – to one's country and its leaders and to one's allies and their leaders. I recall one student who questioned whether he was really obligated to take orders from foreign commanders who might head integrated units to which he found himself assigned. His ultimate loyalty, he insisted, was to the American Constitution, and after that, through a chain of command from the Commander-in-Chief to American commanders. In swearing to uphold the American Constitution he had not explicitly sworn to serve NATO or other international coalitions or agreements. This student was not alone in his skepticism. Many midshipmen, on their initiation day as plebes, have only the faintest idea that in swearing to uphold the Constitution they are pledging to a broader kind of world citizenship. The most compelling rebuttal to their skepticism often came from officers at the Academy who had themselves served in foreign coalitions as part of their military duty in the Persian Gulf and Bosnia. Many were engaged in training other nationals for more cohesive membership in coalitions. Most understood implicitly that patriotism to country is not undermined by broader community allegiances. One can be fervently loyal to country and still serve under or command foreign officers who are part of broader, international coalitions. Marcus Aurelius commanding troops and writing his memoirs today would most likely guard against a patriotism that demands narrow nationalism. For a nation and its military to sever itself from the larger alliance of nations would be an act of self-mutilation—a dismemberment of hand or foot from the body-whole.

The Stoic Hierocles, writing in the first century AD, refers to the notion of cosmopolitanism in the following way: 'each one of us' he describes as 'entirely encompassed by many circles, some smaller, others larger'. 'The first circle contains parents, siblings, wife, and children'. As we move outward, we move through grandparents, to neighbors, to fellow tribesmen and citizens, and ultimately to the whole human race. He insists that it is incumbent upon each of us 'to draw the circles together somehow towards the center', to respect people from the outer circles as though they were from the inner. And we are to do this 'by zealously transferring those from the enclosing circles to the enclosed ones', to bring what is far to what is near, 'to reduce the distance of the relationship with each person'.[7]

Hierocles himself doesn't tell us exactly how we are to psychologically assimilate those in outer circles to inner ones so that we can come to identify with their circumstances. Nor does he explore the nature of our duties, military or otherwise, in terms of which we show respect for others as we move outward in those circles. Later philosophers, themselves influenced by the Stoics, fill out the psychological story. We can do no better than turn to Adam Smith, the 18th century Scottish Enlightenment writer. Sympathy, Smith argues is a cognitive transport, a cognitive moment of becoming another. In his apt words, it involves 'trading places in fancy'. It requires an active transference of the mind onto another, a simulation or role-play of what it is *like to be* another in his or her circumstances. 'To beat time' to another's breast, he says, requires a projective capacity by which we imagine another's case:

> As we have no immediate experience of what other men feel, we can form no idea of the manner in which they are affected, but by conceiving of what we ourselves should feel in the like situation. Though our brother is upon the rack, as long as we ourselves are at our ease our senses will never inform us of what he suffers. They never did, and never can, carry us beyond our own person, and it is by the imagination only that we can form any conception of what are his sensations....It is the impressions of our own senses only, not those of his, which our imaginations copy. By the imagination we place ourselves in his situation, we conceive ourselves enduring all the same torments, we enter, as it were, into his body and become in some measure the same person with him; and thence form some idea of his sensations, and even feel something which, though weaker in degree, is not altogether unlike them.[8]

The description brilliantly presages what contemporary philosophers of mind and cognitive psychologists now refer to as a 'simulation' process, by which we come to identify with others, and in some sense, 'read' their minds. But again, we do well if we go not only forward in time, but backward. Smith was an avid reader of Cicero, (as were most philosophers of the Enlightenment period), and the notion of 'placing ourselves in another's situation' becomes far clearer if we bring to bear Cicero's notion, in *On Duties*, of the different personae we wear.[9] To read another's mind one must 're-centre' oneself on another, by imagining, as Cicero would put it, the shared personae we all have as rational, human beings, but also the personae we wear that are different from person to person. To empathize or simply understand others, we must imagine what it is like to be another with her distinctive temperaments and talents, in her situation and circumstances, living her life with her life choices. It is not just that we 'change' circumstances; we also change who we are in those circumstances. Thus, we don't simply put ourselves in others' shoes. We imagine ourselves *as others in their own shoes*. Sometimes we do this almost unconsciously. But at other times, as Hierocles says, we must 'keep zealously' working at the transference.

We don't tend to think of the contemporary warrior as a 'cosmopolitan' of this sort. But this is a central part of ancient Stoic teaching, and one that current day warriors need to embrace as they increasingly face the demands of international coalitions and long term peace keeping missions in foreign countries. It is a notion we all need to take to heart as the demands of global citizenship become more and more a reality.

Stoicism within the military revives another ancient Greek educational theme – namely, the belief that strong bodies and minds must be cultivated together. Even in leg irons, with a broken leg and in solitary prison, Jim Stockdale forced himself to do more than a hundred sit ups each morning. Controlling his own body, in the face of relentless torture and deprivation, was his way of staying alive and sane. He lived and breathed the Stoic doctrine that effort, endurance and inner virtue are major components of human goodness, and that self-endurance began with gaining control back of his own body, even in shackles.

For a public obsessed with consumption and its consumer products, hungry for epicurean novelties but tired of pleats of adipose, the stripped-down life of military endurance and discipline offers an attractive tonic. Whether at eighteen or fifty, the military officer makes physical discipline a part of his or her daily regimen. It shows up in the unmistakable, steel-gripped handshake, in work-out regimens that begin or end each day, in physical training tests and weigh-ins that are part of one's military record. All my students participated in sports at the end of each day of classes, and most had other additional workout regimens. The retired officers I worked closely with kept up with their training, sporting youthful bodies well into their later years. My office suite mate, retired Admiral 'Bud' Edney, a former pilot and Commander in Chief of the North Atlantic, became an avid 'spinner' with his wife in his retirement years, as well as kept up with his biking and skiing as family activities. Admiral Larson, the four star superintendent of the Naval Academy during my term, had a workout schedule in his home that began each day before 6 a.m. Others who were once submariners and consigned to a treadmill on board, vowed only to run outdoors, however inclement the weather.

For the military, strong bodies are mission critical. The military trains warriors who will have the strength to endure on the battlefield and the stamina to test human limits. Marine bootcamp epitomizes the goal. The eleven weeks of moral and physical training culminates with what is called 'the Crucible,' namely two days of sleep and food deprivation, followed by a gruelling obstacle course in gruelling environmental conditions. Survival is group survival. The goal is for the team to return as a team, even if it means coming home on the back of another.

As civilians, how should we view physical fitness when strong bodies are not exactly mission critical, when there aren't jungles to pass through, daily thirty mile hikes to endure, ammunition and persons and bodies to carry to safety? In most white-collar professions, fit bodies are simply not part of the job description. To have legs of steel and arms of iron is neither here nor there. True, how we look in our clothes might subtly matter for job success, but there is nothing like the ubiquitous (even if unwritten) military requirement to look good in a uniform. But this misses the obvious point. Civilian fitness is mission critical in the very sense that any sort of healthy living requires it. Current worries about the significant rise of child and adult obesity are not misplaced. We need weight that doesn't overly tax vital organs; a strong heart to pump enough oxygen, adequate release of endorphins, serotonin, and other hormones to give us vitality and zest, bones that are dense enough to bear our own weight, and so on.

Ancient Greek and Roman thought is, again, an important source. For Plato and Aristotle, the great Greek philosophers who precede the Stoics, virtue is as much a disposition toward self as toward others, where the care of self includes how we care for our bodies. For example, Aristotle views temperance as a kind of internalized control in which we no longer have excessive bodily appetites and can moderate ourselves without much internal conflict. In short, we have mastered indulgence and its impulses and lost the temptation, as one might say, to do otherwise. The prior developmental step is '*egkrateia*' or self-control or continence. Here we master appetite, but not without active struggle and forbearance. When we lapse from either of these forms of control, we are 'akratic', literally lacking in control or weak-willed. Appetite gets the better of judgment; we know what is best, but act against our knowledge. We avert our eyes. At times, Aristotle and before him, Socrates, suggest that weakness of will is a kind of ignorance.[10] But we do best to think of it as motivated ignorance. We are ignorant only in the sense that we don't want to be reminded of what we know to be best.

Plato's *Republic* has long influenced Western culture in its advocacy of an early education that includes gymnastics as well as music. But Plato insists that in the best education 'the exercises and toils of gymnastics' are not mere 'means to muscle';[11] like music, body building is a way of shaping the psyche as well. For it is a way of building mental discipline and spiritedness, a way of storing the general habit and procedures of control in one's mind as well as in one's muscle memory. The lessons of athletics are wasted, Plato insists, if their point is only to make a body more chiseled or agile. I have heard similar remarks from college athletic coaches who encourage young people to go into sports, not simply so that they can become athletes, but so that they can become individuals who have internalized in a general way the rigors of discipline and self-control. As Cicero remarks, strength of soul resembles 'the strength and sinews and effectiveness of the body'.[12]

In the contemporary world of the military, temperance and bodily fitness are monitored by external judges who test and keep records, who have the power to remove a sailor or marine, if there is a lapse. Some of that surveillance can be harsh and sometimes inadequately sensitive to personal and gender differences. Women's bodies, by nature more fat rich than men's, pose difficult challenges for the military in measuring body fat. Shortly after I left the Academy, a woman who was an exemplary student and recipient of a prestigious prize for an ethics essay was eventually kicked out of the Academy on the grounds that her body fat exceeded the appropriate standard for her height. Even if the charts are different for men and women, the danger in a male culture (especially one that so prizes uniformity and cohesion), is that women will be shoehorned into male moulds. For years, the military struggled to decide what sort of physical fitness requirements to impose on women, given women's different centres of gravity and strength. Standards are now in place that reflect reasonable gender differences, but resentment still lingers among some men that women are getting off the hook too easily. The reply to these complaints, as one of my colleagues at the Naval Academy once said, is simple – ask the man who objects to the women's standards if he would like his acceptable weight range pegged to the women's charts. Silence usually ensues.

In the civilian world, physical fitness and bodily health are more a private matter, and a matter of private virtue. Doctors have always taken records of weight and height, and in recent years, increasingly discuss smoking, diet, exercise and alcohol consumption with patients. But their influence is typically at the level of recommendation rather than requirement. By and large, the disciplined care of one's body sits squarely on one's own shoulders. It is one's own business, like most provinces of morality that fall outside legal purview.

This is as it should be. And yet with one out of two Americans overweight, the virtue of temperance seems to have become a personal virtue that is viewed as optional. 'Self-indulgence is a human condition', Seneca writes, 'even if in some pleasures wild animals are more intemperate than humans'.[13] As with most virtues, temperance is a corrective for a standing human condition – in this case, the tendency toward excessive appetite on the one hand, or bodily neglect on the other. We might add that temperance is also a corrective to overcontrol.

If the Stoics are to offer inspiration, then the lesson to celebrate is not human control in excess, but in moderation. The Stoics are constantly reminding us how and in what way we have more dominion than we might at first think, whether it be in the physical sphere or the moral or emotional arena. But no humanly plausible Stoicism can urge that we have unlimited dominion, even over our own virtue.

Strong characters and strong bodies are part of the military appeal, but so too are manners. For those who believe manners build morals, the military offers the lesson in spades. At the mealtime formation at the Academy, visitors line up daily to see a brigade of crisply pressed uniforms and taut, straight bodies. Officers and midshipmen generally greet civilians with a 'sir' or 'ma'am', locked eye gaze, and firm handshake. They are helpful and courteous, polite and civil. As an ethicist, I came to wonder how deep the surface conduct ran. Do manners lead to morals, etiquette to ethics? Should the civilian world, baffled by the degeneration of civility in public life, take better notice of the role of decorum in military culture? Is good conduct a part of good character?

It is easy to be a skeptic here. Codes of conduct are highly local. What one group finds pleasing and a sign of respect, another may find overly formal or off-putting. Given the variability of conduct codes across cultures, how can behavior that is so culture-specific get to the heart of what matters morally? Moreover, much military conduct is mindless drill and compliance motivated by fear of those higher up in the chain of command. Can motivation so pegged to punishment still help an individual secure inner virtue?

These are legitimate concerns not easily dismissed. They are criticisms most civilians would bring to a military environment, myself included. And yet, I have become persuaded that the military gets it right in thinking that manners matter. Like moral acts such as helping or rescuing, or showing courage or generosity, moral manners are also ways we routinely express our concern or respect for others. To look another in the eye but not stare them down, to listen without interrupting, to be mindful of what would offend, insult, or shame are in many cultures simply the ways we acknowledge others as worthy of respect. True, certain manners may have more local coinage than others. But the fact that codes of etiquette vary culturally and the fact that some codes are morally problematic does not impugn the connection of a good code of etiquette, in general, with morality.[14]

Stoic teachings are again instructive here. Seneca writes a lengthy, seven-book treatise on the subject of how to give favors and receive them. It is a subject we might think, at first blush, as befitting only the interests of a *Miss Manners* and her readership. But as we read On Favours, Seneca shows us how the matter is central to morality and crucial for human fellowship. Even a Stoic, bent on hardscrabble integrity and self-reliance, has an obligation to give gifts and take gifts with grace:

> When we have decided to accept [a gift], we should do so cheerfully. We should express our delight and make it obvious to our benefactor. We must show how grateful we are by pouring out our feelings and bearing witness to them not only in his presence but everywhere.[15]

These attitudes are part of how we care for others and show our gratitude when cared for. Similarly, in *On Duties*, Cicero limns in considerable detail how 'our standing, our walking, our sitting and our reclining, our countenances, our eyes and the movements of our hands' all are the outward expressions of our character.[16] Moreover, the Stoics hold that moral virtue requires a progression that moves from doing actions because they are appropriate and externally in accord with rules of right action, to doing actions that are right because they are motivated by virtue itself. What is mere good conduct in one person can be in another a morally worthy action because of its motivational structure.

However, even if we grant the contribution of good manners to good morals, we might still doubt whether the military is the right model to keep our eye on. Consider Robert Duvall, playing the role of career officer in the film *The Great Santini* (1979). He painfully discovers that he can be the military colonel to his wife and children at home, only at risk of losing them. He takes on the gamble, for he knows no other way of being respected. Reciprocally, one midshipman told me after returning from Thanksgiving break that he was confused at home as to how to address his parents. Should he call them 'Sir' or 'Ma'am' as he does his commanding officers, or just 'Mom' and 'Dad' as he always has? The appropriate forms of respect had become fuzzy in his mind.

The film's notion of respect is based on hierarchy and rank. It is captured by the idea that a military person salutes the uniform not the person, and the uniform higher up in the chain of command. The sight is a common one at the Naval Academy as students with almost mechanically hinged forearms salute officers whom they pass in the yard. Outside the military, respect is typically a more democratic notion. Parents and elders may be deserving of special honour, but all persons, simply as persons are worthy of basic respect. Moreover, respect in the civilian world is often conveyed in caring about the feelings of others, in caring that one not shame or humiliate or slight in so far as such attitudes offend against a person's dignity. This is certainly an underlying theme in Seneca's treatise, *On Favours*. But it is the rare commander who is terribly worried about the nuances of hurt feelings or squashed egos. If anything, most officers would contend that a goodly amount of ego deflation is requisite for strong unit cohesion and achievement of the mission. Finally, there's the nagging issue of appearance, so critical to the military. *Appearing* respectful does matter. Yet why put so much emphasis on the pretence and artifice of behaviour? Why reward the person who may be only a hypocrite or dissembler? Moreover, just how does a straight back or hair pinned impeccably in place actually reflect on the goodness of a soul? In the ladies' room at the Academy, I would see women fix each strand of hair in place with bobby pins and spray so that not a wisp fell below regulation shoulder length. They clearly cared about the well-groomed look of an officer.

But what underlies such care for decorum? Is it really anything other than the desire to please? Both Cicero and Seneca argue that much of decorum is underpinned by a desire to please and to take others' opinions into account.[17] They do not explicitly defend the stance, but they imply that some degree of concern for how one is viewed by others is intimately connected with respect for others. Desiring to be agreeable, to not offend or disdain, to not slight, is part of what is involved in taking another seriously. We ought not to make ourselves servile in the task, or violate our own views of what is morally right in order not to offend. But in cases where there is no conflict, concern for another at the level of emotional and formal comportment seems a part of moral respect for them. Manners matter for this reason.

Even Immanuel Kant, the 18th-century German Enlightenment philosopher, notorious for his austere Stoic-inspired philosophy of duty, urges that duty is not just inner virtue but a matter of manner and affect as well:

> No matter how insignificant these laws of refined humanity may seem, especially in comparison with pure moral laws, anything that promotes sociability, even if it consists only in pleasing maxims or manners, is a garment that dresses virtue to advantage, a garment to be recommended to virtue in more serious respects too.[18]

It is often said that anger is the underbelly of courage, that it mobilizes us to fight, that to be warriors in our lives we need to keep the flame of anger kindled. Cicero rehearses the view: 'no stern commands' can rally ourselves or others, whether on the battlefield or off, 'without something of the keen edge of irascibility'. Irascibility is 'the whetstone of bravery'.[19]

Both Cicero and Seneca will deny the claim. Indeed, the Stoics argue strenuously that anger and rage are, on the whole, pernicious emotions. They do more damage than good. 'No plague has cost the human race more', Seneca says in his famous treatise, *On Anger*. A true Stoic warrior does not rely on anger to fight his battles.

Part of the problem with anger, according to the Stoics, is that it cannot easily be moderated. Once turned on, it cannot easily be turned off. It is a 'runaway passion', the Stoics will say, whose stride outpaces reason and its command. It is 'the most rabid and unbridled of all emotions',[20] says Seneca. It perverts the body and mind, and literally disfigures the face. Seneca is graphic in his portrait. Those who are angry have

> eyes ablaze and glitter, a deep flush over all the face as blood boils up from the vitals, quivering lips, teeth pressed together, bristling hair standing on end, breath drawn in and hissing, the crackle of writhing limbs, groans and bellowing....the hideous horrifying face of swollen self-degradation – you would hardly know whether to call the vice hateful or ugly.[21]

And yet Seneca insists that we can control this hideous frenzy and rid ourselves of its corrosive effects. The method is straightforward, even if bold: let go of the kinds of attachments, to honour or reputation or victory or wealth, which when threatened make us angry. These are not real goods, he teaches following ancient Stoic doctrine. True, the Stoics concede, they are the kinds of goods which we might like to have, which we would prefer rather than disprefer, but having them really does not add anything substantive to our happiness. They are not genuine parts of happiness. For happiness, on the Stoic view (which closely follows Socrates' teachings), is only a function of inner virtue. Its prosperity is the prosperity of virtue, not of wealth, fortune, or the opinions of others.

The full Stoic view may be hard to swallow. We *do* depend on others' opinions of us, and think our reputation and standing in a community matter. We would be different kinds of creatures, far less social and communal, far less able to achieve the very Stoic goals of community and fellowship, if we were totally indifferent to others' praise and blame, compliments or slights. We could not raise children without praise and blame from parents.

Yet in holding that certain emotions, like anger, involve mistaken values, the Stoics presuppose something more fundamental and more revealing: namely, that emotions are themselves kinds of evaluations or appraisals, ways of judging the world. Aristotle too holds that emotions involve construals about the world, though on his position, those construals are neither systematically false nor misleading.[22] They are part and parcel of knowing the world accurately and wisely. This view has been reappropriated by contemporary cognitive psychologists. On that view, emotions involve cognitive assessments of the environment that lead to arousal and desiderative responses. So sadness involves an appraisal that I have been hurt, or love the idea that he is attractive, or pity the thought that someone has suffered unjustly. The Stoics go whole hog, though. Emotions are nothing but beliefs. And consequently, they hold, that we can change emotions in their entirety by changing beliefs. There is no remainder. We might say they are the first to advocate a thoroughgoing cognitive therapy as a method of emotional change. Under their aegis, the particular form that cognitive therapy takes is philosophical dialectic. 'Row the oars of dialectic', Cicero says, if you are to transform the soul.

Few of us hold with the Stoics' view that emotions are nothing but beliefs or as corrigible as them. Nor are we likely to endorse the Stoic doctrine that the kind of beliefs emotions involve are predominantly false, embodying false values. Rather, most of us probably think, with Aristotle and current day cognitive psychologists, that emotions can often give us truthful views of the world, even if sometimes exaggerated or magnified. Also, we tend to think that the desires that lace emotions and the physiological arousals expressive of emotions make for states that are as much body as mind, and hence hard to relinquish by a sheer act of belief or will. Few of us are ready to embrace wholeheartedly the Stoic doctrine that all goods other than the pure goodness of our souls ought to be matters of pure indifference to us, things from which we can fully detach in a search for a meaningful life. And yet despite the harshness of some of their views, the Stoics propound a view with which we are likely to have considerable sympathy – the view that to some degree or other, emotions embody ways of thinking about the world, ways of reading the world and evaluating it. Emotions are a form of judging the world, and when we subtly shift those ways of thinking – namely stop thinking that something is an offence, or a loss, or an injury, or an attraction, we make possible a shift in our emotional states. What most of us probably dispute is that the cognitive shift is itself sufficient for an emotional shift, that feeling can be reduced to believing.

We need to return to the specific Stoic claim that we began with – that anger is an emotion that needs extirpation. Can a Stoic, who roots out all anger, be trained to be killer? Does this feature of a Stoic education make sense for a military person?

The harder conceptual problem, I would suggest, is not in thinking of the possibility of a warrior who lacks anger, but the possibility of a person of virtue who is devoid of all anger. For to be a soldier, defending principle, abiding by rules of engagement, cognizant of the constraints of just war and just conduct in war embodied in such documents as the Law of Land Warfare or the Geneva Conventions, in fact requires a principled response to the demands of warfare. To act out of frenzy or rage, to systematically dehumanize the enemy in the way that anger toward an enemy often requires, for a commander to rev up his troops by blood thirst for revenge, for a pilot to be battle-happy in a way that makes her nonchalant about the 'no-fly' zone – these acts are to risk breaking the moral framework of war. Of course, no one can fight without the adrenaline rush of aggression and competitive spirit and it is a drill sergeant's job in life to push his troops to know those emotions well. But that physiological arousal may not itself be underpinned by the kinds of judgments that Seneca claims ground irascibility and rage.

Even if we can conceive of a warrior who fights best because of principle rather than anger, can we conceive of a true person of virtue who leaves behind a sense of anger, a sense of moral indignation, a sense of outrage? Consider retired Chief Warrant Officer Hugh Thompson, the man some have called the hero of My Lai.[23] On 16 March 1968 he was flying his observation chopper when he spotted several wounded people on the ground, and a dike where a group of GIs approached an injured, unarmed woman about twenty years old, and later one officer prodded the woman with his foot and then killed her. Minutes later he saw dozens of bodies in an irrigation ditch. The writhing movements suggested that some were still alive. American infantrymen on the side of the ditch were taking a cigarette break from battle, and began taking off their steel helmets for a moment of respite. Several minutes later, he saw one of the sergeants shooting at people in the ditch. Thompson's worst fears were confirmed. With his side gunner, Larry Colburn and his crew chief Glenn Andreotta, Thompson landed the bubble, telling Colburn to 'open up ' on the GIs – 'open up on'em, blow 'em away' – if they opened fire at him as he intervened.

The Army, after some thirty years of relative silence, belatedly decorated Hugh Thompson for his valour on that day in My Lai with the prestigious Soldier's Medal. Shortly after, he visited Annapolis for a public address, and we spent some time talking together. What were those moments of sighting the massacre at My Lai like? I asked. What did he feel? In carefully chosen words, he remembered thinking that what he witnessed was too much like Nazi behaviour during the Holocaust. At the time he thought, American soldiers don't behave that way, he said. We don't commit genocide. He had shared similar thoughts with the Midshipmen that day. And the traces of anger and disbelief were still visible in his face and audible in his voice, as he recalled approaching the GIs wielding weapons against the innocents. He himself didn't use the words 'moral outrage.' But it was clear that the judgments he made about the horrors he saw that day were the judgments that constitute moral anger. Thirty years later, upon returning to the village of My Lai for a memorial, he was met by one of the village women who survived the slayings. He remembered her then as a young mother. She was now a frail, aging woman. She yanked at Thompson's sleeve and implored 'why did the American GIs kill my family? Why? Why were they different from you?' He could only break down in tears and say, 'I don't know. I don't know. That is not how I was taught to behave.'[24]

If we follow Seneca, are we consigned to an education that would have forced Thompson to behave differently, to look on with dispassionate disinterest, a kind of Stoic apathy that could incite neither rage nor grief? Would we root out the core of Thompson's virtue and humanity? Seneca himself is inconsistent on the point. Anger is the clear enemy in this essay, and yet he closes his piece with the following exhortation: 'While we still draw breath, while we still remain among human beings, let us cultivate our humanity.'[25] A Stoic, committed to the cultivation of humanity and human fellowship, cannot, in fact, eliminate all human anger. As frenzied and blinding as anger's outbursts, as dehumanizing as rage can be, anger expressed in the right way at the right time is the sure sign of humanity. Aristotle, and not the Stoics, gets this point right: anger can be morally fine and praiseworthy. If the Stoics improve upon Aristotle on this point it is that they remind us that emotions are, more often than we think, a matter of our responsibility. The Stoics urge that the emotions are volitional states. We are not just *affected* when we suffer emotions, but as the Stoics put it, we *yield* or *give assent to* certain judgments implicit in those emotions.[26] Even if we are reluctant to embrace a notion of emotions as voluntary, it is hard to deny that, over time, we have considerable dominion over how we respond emotionally. We take charge of how we cultivate our humanity, including, I would add, our anger.

The Stoics offer important lessons for the military and, I would urge, for civilians as well. They give guidance in how we might begin to shape a character education that takes seriously the values of discipline and self-mastery at the same time recognizing our dependence upon others in small communities, but also more globally.

We have seen that Stoic lessons of self-sufficiency and self-mastery are crucial antidotes to the indulgences of consumerism and appetite that plague the contemporary scene. The point is not to idealize the life of deprivation or slavery (as a Stoic like Epictetus may seem sometimes to do) but rather to cultivate the inner resources and virtues that allow for a measure of control in the face of strong temptations and hard losses. The Stoic wisdom is that we have dominion in more areas of our lives than we often acknowledge. Our physical strength can often be built, our emotions 'affect' us, but we also regulate them and learn habits of mind and expression that convey what we care about.

The Stoics make the latter point by suggesting that proper emotions are forms of judgment that we openly consent to and as it were wilfully 'allow in'. In the case of an emotion like anger, we can control, they say, the judgments to which we consent and endorse. We have seen how this stance has both its attractions and dangers. We know without being card-carrying Stoics that reflection allows us to revise overly hasty views about what may annoy, insult, or offend, and that these revised judgments help us to change how we feel, in some cases releasing us from the grip of unreasonable anger. The Stoics, however, insist that all anger is poisoned and that the truly virtuous person is rid entirely of its venom. But we have argued against the extremism of this view. Anger can also show its face as moral outrage, indignation, and a sense of injustice. There are human moments when anger is precisely the right response, however much we may 'lose' ourselves in the reaction, and similarly so for grief, compassion, and love. Perhaps the Stoic lesson to preserve is that there are ways of recovering our mastery even after we have let go. There are forms of resilience and self-governance that allow for stability in the face of the strongest winds.

The Stoics also insist upon our cosmopolitan status in the world. We are citizens of the universe, not isolated individuals or isolated nations. Military and civic education must emphasize loyalty to country but also loyalty to values that extend beyond national borders. My midshipmen needed to be reminded of their broader citizenship in the urgent circumstance of chain of command: from whom should they take orders? For many of us, the questions of whom to respect or obey and whom to assist are more diffuse. But the young civilian no less than the junior military officer needs to know that moral obligations and wider circles of allegiance must extend beyond national borders. It is not just our economy that is global, but in a pointed way, so is our moral community.

I have turned to the military as something of a case study for exploring Stoicism. And I have done so upon the military's own lead. Many Navy officers I have worked with have implicitly and explicitly embraced Stoicism for guidance. I have argued that we have much to reap from the richness of Stoic texts. But I have also urged a critical attitude in the face of more orthodox, Stoic tenets. The task as moral educators is to shape a Stoicism with a human face. As Coriolanus, Shakespeare's legendary stoic warrior, came to realize, 'it is no little thing to make mine eyes to sweat compassion.'

NOTES

[1] From James B Stockdale, *Courage Under Fire: Testing Epictetus's Doctrines in a Lab of Human Behavior* (Stanford: Hoover Institution Press: 1994).

[2] Epictetus, *Enchiridion*, tr. Nicholas P White (Indianapolis: Hackett, 1994).

[3] For a good discussion of this, see Jonathan Shay, *Achilles in Vietnam* (New York: Simon and Schuster, 1994).

[4] Seneca, *On Anger* II.31, in Seneca, *Moral and Political Essays*, ed. JM Cooper and JF Procopé, (Cambridge: Cambridge University Press, 1995).

[5] As noted in Diogenes Laertius, *Lives of Eminent Philosophers,* tr. RD Hicks, (Cambridge, MA: Harvard University Press, 1972) 6.63. See also Epictetus, *Discourses*, tr. WA Oldfather, (Cambridge, MA: Harvard University Press, 1925, 2.10.3, I.9.2.

[6] Marcus Aurelius, *Meditations* 8.34

[7] See AA Long and DN Sedley, *The Hellenistic Philosophers,* Vol. 1 (Cambridge: Cambridge University Press, 1987), p.349.

[8] Adam Smith, *The Theory of Moral Sentiments*, (Indianapolis: Liberty Classics, 1976 (1759)), 47-8.

[9] Cicero, *On Duties*, ed. MT Griffin and EM Atkins, (Cambridge, Cambridge University Press, 1991). I. 96ff. For a very helpful commentary, see Christopher Gill, 'Personhood and Personality: The Four-*Personae* Theory in Cicero, *De Officiis* I' in *Oxford Studies in Ancient Philosophy* Vol. VI, (Oxford: Oxford University Press, 1988).

[10] See Aristotle's discussion in *Nicomachean Ethics* VII.1-3.

[11] Plato, *The Republic*, tr. GMA Grube, (Indianapolis: Hackett, 1974), Book III.

[12] Cicero, *Tusculan Disputations,* tr. JE King (Cambridge, MA: Harvard University Press, 1927) IV.13 30.

[13] Seneca, *On Anger* I.3, op. cit.

[14] For a lively discussion, see Sarah Buss, 'Appearing Respectful: The Moral Significance of Manners', *Ethics*, 109, July 1999.

[15] Seneca, *On Favours* II.22 in Seneca*: Moral and Political Essays,* ed. JM. Cooper and JF Procopé, (Cambridge: Cambridge University Press, 1995).

[16] Cicero, *On Duties,* I. 128 (using *Cicero: On Duties* ed. MT Griffin and EM Atkins (Cambridge: Cambridge University Press, 1991)).

[17] See for example Seneca, *On Favours,* op. cit., II.1-2, II.13; and Cicero, *On Duties,* op. cit. I.93-124.

[18] Immanuel Kant, *Anthropology from a Pragmatic Point of View*, tr. Mary J. Gregor, (The Hague: Nijoff, 1974), 282.

[19] Cicero, *Tusculan Disputations* IV.19, 21, op. cit.

[20] Seneca, *On Anger,* III.16, op. cit.

[21] Seneca, *On Anger* I.2, op. cit.

[22] See, for example, the account of emotions in Aristotle's *Rhetoric* II.

[23] For my account, I have drawn on the report by Michael Hilton and Kevin Sim in Four *Hours in My Lai,* (New York: Penguin, 1992).

[24] I am remembering the gist of the conversation as it appeared on CBS's *60 Minutes*.

[25] Seneca, *On Anger* III.43, op. cit. For an insightful discussion of *On Anger,* see Martha Nussbaum, *The Therapy of Desire* (Princeton: Princeton University Press,

1994) Chs. 10 and 11.

[26] For a nuanced description of the voluntary and involuntary aspects of emotional experience, see Seneca's *On Anger*, II.1-4, op. cit.

Military Activities and Human Rights

Steve Crawshaw

Much of my subject has already been expressed with enormous clarity, eloquence and compelling debate. While I find it very interesting to learn the degree of consensus, there is much that I would like to pick up on and bring extra ideas and factors to our debate.

There is a subject that at this moment concerns all of us very deeply. Everyone working at Human Rights Watch, or any other human rights organization, thinks and discusses constantly whether a particular war should or should not be fought. But there is an important reason why a human rights organization in general, and certainly Human Rights Watch in particular, stands back. This is sensible, not because we suffer a kind of a moral cowardice and refuse opportunities for standing up and letting ourselves be counted, but because if on any particular issue we were to say, 'Yes, in this case war is acceptable', we compromise our position for subsequent comment and action when the shooting, the bombing and the killing begins. If we supported the idea in principle of a war being fought on a particular issue, then afterwards we may appear to be complaining and only addressing the seemingly narrower points, the points of humanitarian law and the unlawful acts against civilians. Conversely, if we had been against the war, then our voice is less likely to be heard because it seems less relevant. If afterwards we say 'We don't like what is happening here', then people will reply 'well yes, you were against the war in the first place, so of course you are against the idea of civilians being killed'.

The way that the title was presented to me to some extent implies that there is a contradiction between what human rights groups, like Human Rights Watch, are looking for and what military people are look-

---

Steve Crawshaw is the London Director of Human Rights Watch. He joined the *Independent* newspaper at launch in 1986, reporting from Russia, Eastern Europe and the Balkans during the 1989 revolutions, and later, as chief foreign news editor, he covered Burma, China and Southern Sudan.

ing for. In the past the contrast might have well been seen to be that. Had this conference been held at any time in past decades (say fifty years ago for the sake of argument), before groups like Human Rights Watch or Amnesty International existed, there would have been much less consensus. It would be 'you're a bunch of peaceniks', on the one hand and 'you're the people who kill people and don't care' on the other. While we can see a woeful lack of progress in the horrors around us, I believe a noticeable fact is a positive feeling that armed forces within democracies and human rights groups are heading towards a convergent view of a 'proper way' to prosecute these conflicts. For us it is a matter of 'disentangling from the game', to use a sporting metaphor, to act as spectators on the touch line, and not engage in the very hard kicking around the pitch, an activity we have learnt to respect. And yet in a different kind of way, I believe we are useful as well. We do, in the broadest sense, wish the democratic team to win. I like to believe we are now shouting from the touchlines in a useful way, rather than merely complaining, as we have sometimes been seen merely to do in past years.

I would like to pick up the idea of humanitarian law and the way it is practised, and to separate the moral and the practical aspects that seemingly always became very mixed up. The moral perspective can itself quickly be seen as enlightened self-interest. If we start from basic moral precepts, the biblical precept of 'thou shalt not kill' exists basically in every society: we know that killing is not acceptable. However, in some societies killing might be culturally acceptable ('If you've killed my brother, I can kill your brother'), and acceptable revenge killing is codified as law. The idea that you cannot just go around killing anybody is seen in societies across the world as a standard of behaviour. It is a punishable act almost universally.

In war a soldier, by definition, is licensed to kill within those circumstances about which the war has been declared. The two parties both feel that they have the right to shoot each other. However, it is unacceptable conduct to go to the soldier's house, rape his wife and kill his family. Those are the sort of acts which have been with us for hundreds of years, but our attitudes to them have changed very radically within the last century, and at a speed which we often do not ourselves notice.

Changes of technology have altered attitudes as well, and enormously influenced what one can or cannot do. In considering technology, one can elaborate on the case of the air bombing of the Second World War. It is interesting to note that moral attitudes to what is acceptable overlap, to some extent, with the technological possibilities and impossibilities. During the German bombing of Britain and the early stages of the bombing of Germany by the Allies, the main targets were the railway stations and the factories. But even from the start, it was very clear that when you mounted a bombing raid, people who lived in the immediately surrounding area of London docklands or Hamburg docks were bound to be hit as well, however hard you tried to avoid the consequences. It was not seen as being 'unfair': no one would have dreamed of raising that question at the time because it was clear that technology did not permit such accuracy. You dropped bombs as close as possible, and tried to avoid the cathedral and innocent civilians. Towards the end of the war, that fine line had already been crossed. It was accepted that civilians could and would die on a regular basis in bombing. Then, towards the end of the war in 1945, thousands were killed in Dresden in one horrendous night. The plan was to destroy the city, which was full of refugees; the war aim had moved on from factories and stations. The war aim then was to break morale. As military logic it made sense. The Third Reich still refused to surrender, horrific things were happening on the Eastern Front, and the Allies wanted to stop the war. What mattered was to defeat the enemy by whatever means. Much later, of course, such acts were then codified as being completely against the rules. Military acts like those against Dresden, which were already controversial at the time, have since been codified into international law. I would like to believe that nobody at this conference would think that, whatever Saddam Hussein has done, the idea of simply carpet bombing Baghdad and razing it to the ground in the way that Dresden was would not been seen as a useful way forward.

There is a second example of how our views of these things have changed. In June 2002 Human Rights Watch produced a report about organized rape on a truly horrific scale in the Congo war at the moment [September 2002]. There the scale of killing itself is quite extraordinary: two million dead, indirectly or directly, and 300 000 most directly from the military action. Within these events tens of thousands of rapes have occurred. In one town alone we documented that about 2 000 to 3 000 rapes had been committed. The title of our report was 'The War within the War'. Such actions are deliberately used as a way of grinding down the civilian population: the military or non-military leadership have encouraged men in uniform, or in ragged uniforms, or indeed without uniform, to perform such acts. We have seen similar activities in a number of conflicts, such as Rwanda and Sierra Leone, and we are about to produce another report about what happened there and in the Balkans. While being shocked deeply, we became ourselves in some way resistant to the absolute horror.

One should recall a time in living memory, in 1945, when our great ally in the fight against Hitler swept through Eastern Europe. Russia suffered truly horrifyingly from what the Nazis had done, in seeking the complete extermination of particular groups, which went beyond all lunacy of war even by the rules at that time. They sought the mass slaughter of the Slavs, as sub-humans (*untermenschen*), which went way beyond any ordinary sense of how a war should be prosecuted even then. But it was equally shocking to us now, that when the Russian troops came back, they raped on a truly extraordinary scale. This has been documented dramatically, most recently in Antony Beevor's book *The Fall of Berlin 1945* (2002). At the time, the Western Allies did not interfere because it was not quite proper to talk about such matters, together with the fact that we needed those Russians. The idea was 'Well they did suffer terribly themselves, didn't they?' Moscow explicitly permitted ordinary soldiers to think 'How much you have suffered, now go and have your way with those German women'. The democratic governments did not have much of a moral problem with what happened under a dictatorial Soviet regime. We still have whispers of a tacit understanding of such problems.

I first visited the Balkans and Kosovo twenty years ago as a journalism student and have been back regularly over the years and constantly in the last ten to fifteen years. It amazed me that, after the Kosovo war when Milosovic's forces had been driven out, one thought 'Good has triumphed'. Then truly horrific things happened to absolutely innocent Serbs, who were known to have been personally very brave in speaking out against bad things in the past. They too suffered violence. The West, for a dismayingly long time, thought, 'Ah well the Albanians suffered so much over such a long period, it's fair enough that they should go and kill a few Serbs, now that the war is over. We had better turn a blind eye'. I think that such a notion that somehow one act justifies another is deeply worrying. Asymmetry does not excuse such acts, however badly the other side is behaving. The Twin Towers destruction does not justify unlimited counter-acts that, so to speak, fall outside every moral radar screen.

In practical terms one is nevertheless often left with a completely unsolved problem. I would like to believe that, probably, there would be a shift in the thinking now of many of the same British Army officers at the time of Bloody Sunday thirty years ago. I think that, whatever happened then, we can now take a long view of the context of *how* it happened. Whatever the fears of the soldiers on ground, whatever the horrific brutality, the act of throwing away the rulebook was lamentable. In one sense, the definition of a terrorist is that he or she has knowingly thrown away the rulebook. The feeling of 'We are surrounded, these guys are doing this, we have to somehow get back at them', became fourteen civilian deaths on one day. For all the psychological reasons, what was going on in those local people's heads, and the soldiers' heads, and their immediate commanders' heads, was the idea that we need to get back at them somehow' and 'we're not quite sure what's going on'.

Of those fourteen deaths I suspect there will probably not be very much disagreement in this conference. Prime Ministers John Major and Tony Blair were able to distance their policies, pick up and take matters forward later. Bloody Sunday acted as a recruiting sergeant for the IRA and everything else that followed was poisoned for years. When I was writing about Bloody Sunday two years ago, I went back to the Colindale Library (the British Library's Newspaper Library), and looked through all the papers from that period. In the *Belfast Telegraph* for 30 January 1972 I read words to the effect that 'We've had difficult years in 1970 and 1971, but we feel we're just about to turn a corner. Let's hope that 1972 will be the year where we can think we're reaching normality again, we can somehow talk to each other and move forward'. It was heartbreaking for me to read such genuine sentiments of hope knowing what happened so soon afterwards.

Russia has been my subject for many years and I have watched that country with astonishment and sometimes delight. I am much more optimistic about Russia than many people are. It is still often perceived as simply a place of complete lawlessness, which is not true: things are moving and improving. If one looks at the big picture one can see that the metaphysical 'political stock market' has changed. With its ups and downs, life has got better and better over the last ten to fifteen years. Chechnya, however, is a truly extraordinary phenomenon. The Russian Government is a democratically elected government. While it believes in the rule of law, it does not believe that human rights really matter in Chechnya. I have seen with my own eyes this extraordinary sense of another Bloody Sunday writ large. To be fair, Bloody Sunday is like nothing in comparison with Chechnya, where people 'disappear' in military custody every day. They are killed by Russian soldiers day after day, week after week, and it is not just the rebels but ordinary civilians. In a gross distortion, the Russians now claim that their actions against Muslim terrorists are part of the wider war on terror in the post-11 September environment.

There are indeed terrorists in Chechnya today, but there are many many more terrorists than there were a few years ago. I can remember Russians and Chechens crouching together, Chechen neighbours weeping bitterly and angrily for a dead Russian who had died trying to save a Chechen neighbour's life and been shot by Russian troops. These examples illustrate a sense of bonding together against the madness of authorities, who in that context were behaving entirely brutally and undemocratically. Indeed, in their battle against the terrorists they achieved no military objectives and fatally undermined any democratic legitimacy now and for the future.

Finally, in elaboration of points that Ambassador Pierre-Richard Prosper raised it was gratifying that Human Rights Watch, my organization, was quoted in glowing terms several times with our documented horrors of the Saddam Hussein regime in Iraq. We try very hard in all our reports to document all incidents and statistics within legal parameters very, very carefully. I was glad that he did pay tribute to the importance of international justice, but it is startling that the most important tool of international justice, the International Criminal Court, is not subscribed to by the US. The ICC is a universal institution that can fortify and buttress global civil society against lawlessness, either of wicked regimes or hideous terrorists.

I was also interested in the question that came up on the Northern Alliance in Afghanistan, where we are working on a document to inquire into incidents and accidents. There seemed to me to be an undertone of not quite wishing to confront the truth and dwelling on the difficulties of knowing in advance about possible breaches of law and universal morality. Thus my final conclusion is that whitewashing over problems afterwards helps nobody, either in the short or long term. It can never be justified in democracies. Playing strictly by the rules matters most of all when others are not themselves doing so.

Discussion

Asymmetries of force

The morality of military force used against those who have offended you can be asymmetric in both scale and proportion. General counter-terrorist action from long range, for instance in the use of precision bombing from 50,000 feet against known 'targets', is likely to be categorically different from the action taken personally by members of the security forces against individual terrorists. This emphasizes the cool detachment of planners and pilots, which seemingly gives them the luxury of moral protection well away from the actions or atrocities committed by terrorists, a luxury often not shared by opposing armed forces on the ground. Collateral damage from long-range weaponry will, of course, cause widescale resentment amongst those on whom the weapons fall, often far outweighing any atrocities committed by terrorists elsewhere and at different times. A principle is a principle that should be maintained: questions of scale are usually of a different (philosophical) category-order. Acts against terrorists should be always based on precision targeting, so accidental harm to others in the community or vicinity can be reduced to the absolute minimum.

In more widescale military action and war, precision is no less morally desirable. The moral difficulty is emphasized when those engaged on one side see their activities as warfare legitimately fought with the weapons of terror, inducing acute psychological fear, and on the other side, those countering terror with armed force. Terrorism on one hand and incipient war on the other have to be distinguished and moral asymmetries recognized.

The difference between accidental and deliberate killing is, of course, crucial to the moral debate. For instance, air power is a relatively cheap and comparatively effective instrument. The few civilians killed in air strikes in the last ten years have been putatively, but favourably, compared with the likely casualties had armies been engaged in fighting backwards and forwards through those same villages and towns. Bombing such targets as in the Tora Bora area in Afghanistan to deal with Al-Qa'ida fighters might appear the most effective means but, being unsubtle, may well produce much collateral damage. The best way to deal with any accidental physical or unpredicted moral damage is immediately to own up to the mistake, promise every sort of compensation and then deliver it. Any attempt to deny an incident, or mistake, or deny any responsibility, is morally dangerous. The well-publicized incident of the wedding party in Afghanistan caught in a US air strike is a case in point. Instantaneous expressions of regret would have greatly mitigated the adverse moral opprobrium, even if the dead could not have been brought back to life.

Moral asymmetries

Governments and those in authority of course have the moral duty to protect their own people from taking personal risk. Asymmetric technical means, involving less or minimal risk to those fighting a 'war against terrorism', reveal further moral asymmetries that can be used for propaganda purposes against security forces. Terrorism is not just a band of people waging war by another means, it is about political and cultural grievance. Military action against terrorists should be confined to 'keeping the lid on the boiling pot', while politicians and civil authorities act to solve real causes of the terrorists' grievances. Air power, effective in one way, can never get to the root cause of the problem. Identifying and killing terrorists still does not solve the root cause either: successfully engaging in confidence building with society does, in the long-term. Since 11 September 2001, some Western democracies have sought to limit civic freedom in order to contain terrorism with practical measures. This is dangerous, however governments cannot just let terrorism occur and spread unchecked. They have to consider all such freedoms and the acuteness of danger to them, before circumscribing any of them. If in doubt, then there is justification to wait and only restrict freedoms further if there is more evidence against guilty parties, or fresh events occur, to prove beyond peradventure, that one is right so to do. Theoretically, for long-term posterity, you need to be quite sure that your action, whether military force or legal restriction, is justified – absolutely and without doubt. Pre-emptive action in 'imminent danger' is justified, but you must always stand on the right side of right and wrong.

By definition, it is never easy to make moral judgements. Agents of military power range from the gun-toting twelve year-olds in Uganda or

Sierra Leone, trained, ready to use their weapons and accepted by passers-by, in contra-distinction to airmen dropping 'daisy-cutter' bombs recently in Afghanistan, also doing their duty. One is 'philosophical' about distinguishing between such persons and their motives.

Answers also have to be found, post-11 September 2001, to questions about 'stoicism' versus anger, and reason being the 'slave of the passions' (David Hume). There are arguments that anger is justified and appropriate in order to mobilize and motivate troops in battle. It is not appropriate however, for a pilot to be motivated by a sense of individual revenge. Anger, when appropriate, should not blind the person so that other human emotional and reasonable responses are eliminated. Philosophers David Hume and Bertrand Russell suggest that emotions should 'school reason'. The neurologist Joseph Ledoux, author of *The Emotional Brain*, suggests that anger is a primitive emotion, because it goes to the brain straight from sensory input without going through the neo-cortex, as many of our other emotions do. Primitive emotions are categorically hard to control or to mediate through judgement and reason; they are 'runaway passions'. Reason should always contribute to motivation, in the Aristotelian sense of forming our habits, aims and objectives.

Military duty

Those opposing the West feel angry and impotent. They feel that they are slaves to the West and its technology; their anger can easily get out of control. While understandable, their actions taken in anger are not justifiable if they contravene universal norms and laws. It cannot be ignored that human vulnerability and broad injustices abound in too many parts of the world. There is a right to grieve, to be angry, but it is better patiently to avoid an angry obsession. That is the nature of stoicism as a universal ethical principle and pattern of behaviour. It certainly seems that the stoic warrior ideal should apply to persons in the West and particularly Americans in the current debate.

Honour is undoubtedly part of the military ethic. General Sir John Hackett, in his book *Profession of Arms* (1963), asserts that a sense of honour is an essential basis to justify a 'right cause' and the use of military force by a democratic country. 'Honours' are different from 'honour'. They have to be earned by recognition of other people. Once given, they are still goods that can be snatched away from individuals. 'Honour' in the Socratic view, is something intrinsic, of the inner-person, linked to character and integrity. Nevertheless there will always be an ambivalence and tension between outward esteem and inner self-sufficiency.

Stoic philosophy also has been the philosophy of revolution, of anti-conventionalism, of power and freedom. It also tells us what should *not* govern our actions: we should concentrate on those goods that are within our power, and not be angry or aggrieved by those things that are not in our power to attain. Another aspect of stoicism is that a person is responsible for those things he or she can influence. The Stoics' anti-conventionalism and counter-intuitive stance also paves the way to the Kantian view of 'willing' something to happen, as the proper basis for morality.

Human fear and loathing against terrorists who are blowing up your people is of course wholly understandable, but a balance must be sought. Willing to win seems to be the way the current Sharon government in Israel works, ignoring too often otherwise normal, sensible rules put forward for maintaining the moral basis of the use of force against terrorists and the stoicism of the professional soldier. Politically, end-state idealism has an edge over practical and immediate heavy-handed pragmatism, as had been shown over forty years of progress, however fragile, in Northern Ireland. Long-held grievances can take very many years to be effectively mitigated and set right, politically and culturally. The sheer lack of understanding, of which we are all guilty in numerous situations of conflict around the world, causes many of the moral problems for any sort of effective intervention, however altruistic. The intervention in Rwanda (1994) was, of course, an instance of naïvety and bad faith.

Some circumstances and events over which we do have control can also be short-sighted, such as the West's policy of arming Saddam Hussein and the Mujahadeen resistance fighters in Afghanistan in the 1980s. Historical memories can be very long; the history of the Balkans is a case in point. The relevance of the battle of Kosovo Polje (1389) is still claimed as a cause of continuing tension and violence to the present day. An accurate sense of history is important, but it is much more important to let go of a sense of grievance, and not continue to perpetuate it. The truth about Bloody Sunday in Londonderry (1972) may assist in this process, but this may take a very long time. The International Committee of the Red Cross found recently, after interviewing 20,000 victims of many conflicts around the world, that psychological wounds always persist. Events of sixty years ago are as if yesterday for the Chechens, for the Jews, for the Palestinians. So are many myths of sixty, or even six hundred years' 'currency'.

Chapter 5

Means & Ends – Stabilization *Post Bellum*

Relief – A Human Right

Roger Yates

We have heard from both British and American government speakers that Afghanistan was a success and that they were proud of what had been achieved. But has stabilization really been a success?

I am not sure. Stabilization is not merely a matter of moving from bombs to bread. It is much more complex. Warlord, rather than democratic, politics continues. Warlords still control their territory and finances. There still remains a lack of political will by the international community, including the British government, to expand the International Security Assistance Force (ISAF) throughout the country, or even in the North around Mazar-i Sharif, where it would be most useful. A lot of funding is being pledged and delivered, but most is still being spent on emergency relief work. People want development aid, but the money is not yet reaching the villages for that purpose. Stabilization is not just a matter of survival.

The causes of conflict are many. In Afghanistan land ownership is hugely unequal. In one village we visited, fifteen families owned all the land that was to sustain two hundred families. That is not a condition for long term stabilization. Without moral, political and financial commitment to stabilization, there is some doubt about retaining the moral high ground when solving practical and immediate problems. The morality of causing further suffering needs to be considered, while planning for an attack on a country, in Iraq or elsewhere. The humanitarian consequences should be seriously factored into the decision whether to attack or not, as well as all the legal considerations. The fundamental question is: can there be just cause for war without preconditional moral consideration given to stabilization afterwards?

Roger Yates is Head of Emergencies at Action Aid and as a member of the UK NGO-Military Contact Group has been involved in raising awareness of the problems of humanitarian aid. An engineer by profession, he spent 16 years working as development and emergency programmer in Africa, Asia and the Caribbean.

Being so very expensive, effective stabilization relies on many external factors for the repair of devastation, including the return of international trade. During the conduct of a war, the damage done will have long–term consequences for the process of stabilization. Governments, Non-Government Organizations (NGOs), military and the UN share great responsibilities, and NGOs are not merely camp followers. We consist of a broad range of organizations. We have to work together, yet sometimes we have to restrain our activities. Restraint is not only for civilian organizations. For instance the military, motivated by moral duty and with a capability of giving relief aid, might be better off suspending that activity, while others take over the task – being better equipped, experienced and demonstrably motivated by impartiality and humanitarianism.

NGOs are of course independent and not part of the same political project as the military actors in a conflict. Preserving humanitarian access and relief, we attempt to attain recognizable standards in our work. We are not merely giving charity. We maintain that humanitarian relief is a basic 'human right' and try to deliver that 'right' as far as we possibly can, or push others to fulfil it. NGOs are also involved in promoting development – in people and of opportunities. Possibilities for change that emerge during conflict can be greater than at any other time. Any human development hitherto would have been greatly dependent on existing power structures that the West will have altered. Giving relief can indeed be 'empowering' to those who previously had no power: simultaneously village democracy can be developed, changing society for the better. Frequently NGOs are involved in promoting participation, empowerment of poorer people, in building the capacity of people to cope in the future. Other NGOs work on peace and reconciliation directly.

The military's role in stabilization is rather different. Their task is to deliver and uphold security, not just from a military point of view when the shooting stops, but understand what the people they are protecting consider to be 'security'. The military should arrange their work and mandate around that. Security sector reform, training of new armies and police forces, are also important roles for the military. If military forces do get involved in delivering relief, they have to recognize that it might undermine independent humanitarian relief on the basis of 'need' which is seen to be not politically motivated. The military do not have the skills to deliver relief in the most effective way, however efficient in the short-term.

Finally, the military have to be careful when they are attempting to coordinate their activities and those of NGOs. Military accountability to their chain of command is one thing. Accountability to those people to whom relief is delivered can be more effectively and sensitively achieved by NGOs. We are currently doing much work in developing understanding and promoting that accountability to those we are serving, in the long-term.

Humanitarian Space

Jean-Michel Piedagnel

It is important to deny, or even strangle, the idea that all NGOs are all the same, that all those working in the humanitarian community are one. I shall do it by explaining the state of development and the operational concepts Médecins Sans Frontières (MSF) has achieved in providing its service over many years. MSF needs an autonomous 'space' or frame of action. There are three basic criteria to meet this hypothesis. We need the freedom and ability to conduct proper dialogue with those we want to help, without the presence of those who control them, such as the government or military faction. Secondly, we need to have the freedom to circulate and evaluate the needs of the people. That is not easy in areas of conflict: we do not expect full security, just effective freedom to circulate. Thirdly, we need the ability to verify that the assistance we have delivered has reached the population we want to help.

This appears very simple in theory; in practice it is very complicated. A minimum standard is what we seek, case by case. In Angola recently, we discovered that we could only speak through a military translator, seeking the verification we needed. Surprisingly the process worked: we felt that the assistance of food and health had been delivered to the right civilians. MSF, however, has had to withdraw from North Korea, because the three minimum criteria were not met. The food we have been delivering did not reach the most needy, despite a massive multinational operation we had set up in that country. The food was helping the very regime that caused starvation. 'Humanitarian space' was denied us. Establishing room for people to develop best their own humanity is our first priority and major responsibility, not merely to deliver medical assistance.

Jean-Michel Piedagnel joined the UK office of Médecins Sans Frontières as Executive Director in 2001 after a commercial career in international trade. He has worked as s field volunteer, managing programmes in Sierra Leone, Lebanon, Nigeria, Angola, Burundi and Montenegro.

The policy of stabilizing a country will inevitably have a political agenda. It might not, however, coincide with fulfilling the real needs of the people. Indeed MSF might not want to associate itself with that policy. Our 35 years of practical experience has taught us to define and adhere to certain principles, and practices – impartiality, neutrality and independence. Neutrality and impartiality, seemingly straightforward, can become confused. Impartiality means non-discrimination according to race, religion or any other division, as well as adherence to the basic requirement of proportionality 'according to need', as defined by the Red Cross.

We have made assessments in Israel and Palestine, for example. In the aforementioned country we find no needs that MSF can meet, although I must emphasize our absence is not politically motivated. Working in Palestine we maintain our neutrality by taking no part in the conflict. Sometimes, however, we do speak out impartially, when we see things that we consider wrong – unlike the Red Cross who never make judgements on any situation. This illustrates that we are not all the same in the humanitarian community.

Independence of spirit and action is strictly adhered to. This often causes much criticism of MSF. We are seen not to want to comply with others and their policies, for instance in a post-conflict stabilization plan. Independence also means financial independence. We rely mainly on voluntary donations and we have found our independence is recognized and upheld by the flow of donations. It continues to work, after 35 years of adherence to the principle.

Involved in the peace process in Sierra Leone in 1997, we had to negotiate with 'peacekeeping' Nigerian troops, who were actually more involved in fighting the rebels than peacekeeping, in order to gain access to rebel-held territory. It worked: our intentions were indeed recognized by the Nigerian commander, who understood that we merely wanted to help civilians. But UN troops operating in 'blue berets' made no progress in restoring peace after years of bitter fighting. The British intervention in 2000, however, saved the country from further war and stabilized it. Everyone saw there was no big political or military agenda behind the British intervention. It was relatively simple. While the roots of the conflict may still remain in Sierra Leone, MSF and other NGOs wish to continue to address the causes in the practical ways we perform best. If we are seen to be doing other things, we might be denied access to the population. The local people's 'perception' of external actors operating within their country is significant.

How can NGOs help governments, politicians and military to deliver the peace dividend? We cannot get involved in politics. It would compromise our 'humanitarian space' and operating principles, impartiality, neutrality and independence. The 'peace process' must be a political process. It usually involves strong political and military agendas, with which we do not want to be associated. Do not misunderstand me; this is not a value judgement of the peace process, or even the 'purpose' of a war. Nor am I critical of other NGOs, who rightly have their own principles, roots and histories.

Finally we do not believe that the military can really deliver and sustain 'humanitarian' intervention. They can do 'relief work'. Governments may take control, through the military, of an area and try hard to promote the norms of humanitarian law and human rights, as well as take care of the people. This is not the same as humanitarian work, in MSF's view. The language is very important. The military can seldom really take on full responsibility for populations. Propaganda and political spin will always be suspected. The 'bombs to bread' motive in Afghanistan seems to many NGOs to be short-term political 'spin', to justify the intervention.

Stabilization – For Real People

Tim Aldred

Stabilization is clearly a very complex process, in the sense that I believe it is harder to manage peace than it is to get to peace in the first place.

In May 2002 I was in a Tamil Tiger area in Sri Lanka, reviewing some of the work in support of the Church and meeting some members of the communities we assist. At that point the ceasefire had been in place for some months, there was quite an air of cautious optimism. People were very pleased that bombs were no longer falling on their heads and there was a feeling things were getting better. But talking with the poorer communities, fishermen and internally displaced people in 'displacement camps' revealed a more complex picture of what was actually happening to these poorer groups of people. The front lines were open to trade for example, in fish, seafood and vegetables. Fish, as food, was being transported across front lines and being sold in the South. Markets had opened up and in the long run people could see that life could be good. In the interim, however, a sudden rise in demand doubled the price of some basic commodities, for example rice. Poorer communities, who did not have land and were reliant on cash were actually finding it significantly harder to pay for basic daily needs and to keep their families going. Paradoxically, the peace in some ways had made things worse.

Another example of the anomalies of peace restoration can also be found in Sri Lanka. Medical staff had been working throughout the war period in many isolated hospitals for very low wages. They stayed because there was nowhere else for them to go. Following the ceasefire they had freedom, they had the chance to seek better jobs elsewhere. For whatever

---

Tim Aldred has worked in many countries as a water supply expert. From 1998 he has worked with the Catholic Agency for Overseas Development (CAFOD) as Emergency Co-Financing Officer for humanitarian aid projects particularly in Serbia, North Korea, Zimbabwe, Mozambique, Sri Lanka, the Democratic Republic of the Congo, El Salvador and Afghanistan.

reason, however, the system did not work quickly enough to give them a proper salary and benefits for the work they were doing. So a lot of staff had actually left those hospitals and the health service suffered considerably as a result of the peace.

Clearly these issues I have just mentioned can be resolved and indeed people are working to resolve them. But for me it was an interesting demonstration of the complexity of stabilization processes, and the need for very careful analysis and investment to make the peace work. We have already heard of problems about funding stabilization in Afghanistan. I believe the dynamic is that often the immediate humanitarian aid providers solve the problem from their perspective, then pack up and go home. The development–funding agencies have other priorities. They need eighteen months to set up their resources on the ground before things can start to happen in terms of sustainable development. This, I assure you, is not an over-generalization.

Drawing my first lesson from experience, I believe what is happening in Afghanistan at the moment is the mismatch of funding and strategic planning: it is of great concern because it is destabilizing. Kofi Annan in his speech last week stated, 'Donors have not followed through sufficiently on their commitments to help with reconstruction, rehabilitation and development.' And he goes on to warn that if this is not addressed, the Afghan people will lose hope. Desperation breeds violence. So I think there is room for improvement on planning for stabilization and sustainable development, and how we genuinely address the first years of post-conflict rebuilding. A genuinely 'joined-up approach', with good analysis to take us through what can be a very difficult period, is vital. There must be a sincere commitment to stay in the country, even though the television cameras have gone.

My second theme is about military involvement in the distribution of humanitarian aid and to expand on why, for us, it is an issue that is of considerable difficulty and debate. My best example is where actually there has been no actual foreign military intervention. We support quite a significant feeding programme across Zimbabwe, and in one location earlier this year, we were feeding approximately 40,000 individuals. Elements among the war veterans association began to believe that the aid that we were providing had a political motive, that it was effectively in support of the opposition Movement for Democratic Change (MDC). Their concern led them effectively to force the suspension of the work that we were doing for a time. It was known that we were a United Kingdom agency: the tension between the United Kingdom and Zimbabwe governments obviously had an effect on our operation. We needed to go through quite a careful and difficult process of negotiation to demonstrate our genuinely apolitical and humanitarian credentials. Our generous donor, the Department for International Development (DFID), actually helped us considerably by wisely maintaining a very low-key posture and helping us to protect our position as a humanitarian and apolitical organization, not one that was closely linked to any government. And I am pleased to report at the end of the story, that we were able to resume work. In the interim, of course, those children who we should have been supporting risked going hungry. All of this emphasizes the moral problems, particularly since it was not at all certain that there would be other agencies that could step into the breach.

If that moral tension is so problematic when we are in a non-conflict situation, how much more so when we are all working in a conflict or post-conflict situation? If I arrive in a village in Afghanistan at some point in the near future, will the community understand me when they realise that I am British? Will they think 'is this person a peacekeeper', or 'is this someone related to a combat role', or 'is he a humanitarian aid worker'? I can foresee confusion and it becomes even more confusing when the military strategy is labelled a 'humanitarian strategy', as was the Kosovo War (1999). The reason why these tensions and confusions need to be reduced and eliminated is that they inevitably impact on our collective ability as people of good will not only to meet the 'rights' of civilians caught in war or recovering from war, but also to meet those rights to basic needs, namely water, food, livelihood, healthcare and development.

I emphasize that the moral imperative with which we are all concerned in preserving the rights of civilians affected by war, relates before and during, not only after conflict. The subtitle 'from bombs and bullets to bandages and bread' is misleading. As NGOs we are not in the bombs and bullets business at any point. We do not simply turn up at the end; we are engaged *throughout* a conflict. Our concern is to retain enough of a humanitarian framework, which includes 'space' for humanitarian action to take place. If we succeed, that maximizes the ability to support communities affected by war, no matter where they are in relation to a 'front line'.

My third point is that our ability to affect stabilization happens as a consequence of early decision-making, not simply in the post-conflict period. It is influenced, as we have already heard, by the decision to go to war in the first place. Is the destruction really necessary? It is a lot easier, for example, to keep, maintain and support an existing hospital than to build and completely equip a new one. If your reasons for going to war are just, and perceived as such by those then trapped in the middle of a conflict, are you really going to be welcomed when you offer your humanitarian services only in the recovery phase? People do have long memories. I remember, when I lived in Kabul, having a conversation with a cobbler who had a small business on the corner of the street near my residence. When he realized I was British, he made it clear that this caused him some difficulties. And he said that ever since the British installed 'that puppet governor' in the 1840s, 'we've never really liked you'. The decisions that we make now often have an impact well into the future.

In relation to stabilization, even if your war is a just one, your just cause can be undermined by a failure to respect 'right conduct' in the use of force, legally and morally. From a stabilization point of view, if you have offended during the war, will you be respected in the post-conflict phase when you arrive and say that you are offering your services to contribute to recovery? Agencies inevitably have become linked to the policies of governments, and the Catholic Agency For Overseas Development (CAFOD) is a British aid agency, which affects the ways in which we as United Kingdom aid workers are perceived and the extent to which we too are trusted. That means being seen to be correct and fair with respect to direct action as well as indirect, such as the prisoners held at Guantanamo Bay. It means being scrupulous about the practice of war, in decisions to use particular types of weaponry, fuel-air bombs and the like. These decisions will matter when we reach the stabilization phase.

Finally, why does stabilization matter? Why is it a moral question? It matters because at the end of the day stabilization is about real people and real lives. The moral imperative for us is to protect life and to restore normal, fulfilling livelihoods to those civilians that find themselves, through no fault of their own, affected by war.

Discussion

Humanitarian Integrity

The December 2001 report by the International Commission on Intervention and State Sovereignty, set up by the Canadian government at the request of the UN Secretary General, suggested that the term 'humanitarian intervention' be changed to the 'responsibility to protect'. NGOs have a difficulty with the notion of 'humanitarian' bombs and bullets.

'Protection' is a word that is much wider in meaning than 'security'. NGOs can provide protection too. The word 'humanitarian' has lost much of its meaning and 'humanitarian space' implies continuing 'victimhood' in an area. The 4 500 villages destroyed by Saddam Hussein, for instance, have been rebuilt by their own peoples. The claim remains that 'humanitarian space' is to do with freeing peoples. The case of Somalia (1993) was particularly unfortunate because the 'peacekeepers' came in, became peace-enforcers and then left.

Accepting government funding does indeed compromise the perception of NGOs' political independence. Working with local people directly can mitigate adverse expectations. People gaining assistance as a right enables misunderstanding to be diminished further, and this can be achieved by an NGO working with other NGOs to begin urgently needed work on the spot and to demand funding to meet it. In former Yugoslavia, large-scale funding from governments was absorbed into the stabilization process through NGOs. The NGOs remained, and had to negotiate with those left in power, without being seen either to cooperate or collaborate with them, and so losing their independence. Nevertheless, the NGOs were still associated with military intervention.

On the wider subject of funding, a number of British humanitarian NGOs receive it from the British government. Thus, as we have already heard, CAFOD's involvement in Zimbabwe is seen by the war veterans as having political strings attached, however altruistic is DFID. Oxfam receives more that fifty per cent of its money from the British government: it is difficult to think of it otherwise than an arm of policy, however benevolent.

On the question of accountability and speaking out about political agendas of governments, MSF is in a good position because of its private funding base. To an extent, UK charities are hampered in what they can say because of the charity laws and regulations on the political activities of registered charities. Many charities, however, have policy teams routinely finding ways of influencing and holding governments to account. There is a fine balance and compromise to be achieved between these two factors in the stabilization process. NGOs are additionally faced with the need to watch that intervention does not get out of hand, particularly in planning in advance of military operations. Since NGOs have their own moral duty to take account of consequences in advance of the war starting (in order to plan their own aims, activities, financial investments in the short, medium and long term), it seems sensible that they ought to have direct contact with political and military planners. This somehow has to be attained without compromising independence, impartiality and neutrality. A greater understanding in Britain between NGOs and the military has been achieved over the past few years, by good dialogue and consultation as well as a number of practical joint training exercises.

Cooperation and Consensus

A good degree of cooperation can be achieved short of collaboration. In a UN-mandated mission joint understandings are particularly necessary. NGOs cannot get too close to the military and exchange information, which can become 'operational intelligence'. Each side has to be as effective as possible in its duties and there have to be compromises and cooperation. There are, however, considerable differences between a fully belligerent set of operational circumstances and peacekeeping. Exchange of information must be a matter of judgement at the time.

British military doctrine has developed three principles in Peace Support Operations (PSO) to make provision for stabilization. They are consent, impartiality and the use of force. Consent is a variable, the line between peacekeeping and peace enforcement. Moving to 'war fighting' is crossing the line of impartiality. A more judicial use of force beyond self-defence, as was suggested by events in Rwanda (1994) and Srebrenica (1995), has been allowed in order to prevent acts of genocide, for example. Taking doctrine formulation further, three concepts in a spectrum of activities are being developed: implementation, stabilization and normalization. Conflict prevention and conflict resolution are military ends, but both work towards normalization.

Often a very large number of the population in a country suffering conflict have psychologically lived through circumstances and events of brutality and violence. One thinks of the Congo and Indonesia particularly in recent years. Instability in one nation can cross the border to others. It is difficult for a new government, or a 'cleansed' government in a 'stabilization' phase to bring people to court. Is it the peacekeepers' responsibility, or that of the International Criminal Court (ICC) when it is established fully? There is no immediate answer to this question.

Sometimes NGOs can fall into the habit of moral self-indulgence and feel they are not subject to practical norms. The military, mandated to be responsible for a particular area, may not be any less 'morally' motivated. Some NGOs, claiming to be entirely free standing, can cause accidental damage or disaster with consequences far beyond the immediate area or time-scale. The more NGOs emphatically do not see themselves working in a vacuum, the more coordination can be achieved according to a well-defined plan and code of conduct. That coordination, however, must fall short of military control. The mutual understanding between the mandates of military forces and individual NGOs is of the greatest significance.

In respect of NGOs monitoring countries suffering internal conflict, one often finds local armed forces and police have committed terrible atrocities over many years. Indonesia is a case in point. Often NGOs do not want to get involved or be part of the process; or indeed they might not be accepted because of individual NGO's narrow focus, which may be thought to be aligned to the terrorists' agenda. Most NGOs work in extremely difficult environments and it is very hard for their members to avoid emotional involvement. NGO accountability certainly needs to be improved.

In summary, consensus between all external parties helps to promote stabilization in a country that has suffered conflict. Enabling people to think and act for themselves is equally important, while at the same time preventing one despotic government merely being replaced by another. International law is a universal basis for developing our world and countering a new and real enemy since 11 September 2001. Individuals in many other countries have the same aspirations as is normal in Western democracies, and this is the basis for all moral consensus. All agencies, governments, military and NGOs, need to work even harder in future – towards the single, ultimate aim of achieving a more equitable and just world.

Chapter 6

Military Ethics: Questions for a New Chapter

Military Ethics: Questions for a New Chapter

Patrick Mileham

Language

Before and during the Cold War, moral questions in the context of military operations relied on political and legal interpretation, and seemed to be of little direct interest to Britain's armed forces. The British Army's professional code was implicit, comprehensive, long-understood and passed on through the generations by Sandhurst and Woolwich, the regimental system and general osmosis of the decencies in an otherwise rough occupation. The Royal Navy and Royal Air Force had similar ways of inculcating professional conduct. None of these processes and understandings, however, were connected in the minds of those in uniform with general moral philosophy. On the other side of the Atlantic, the veteran US commander General Maxwell Taylor gave his view of military ethics as the Cold War drew to a close, '...there are no official texts or authoritative codes to which to refer, and possibly there never will be'.[1]

One truth that the British armed forces have discovered since 1989 is that the traditional pragmatic approach may not be sufficiently comprehensive or subtle to cope with the surprises of modern-day military operations, or more widely, problems of security. Military pedagogy has progressed in leaps and bounds and many newly codified constituents of 'the military art' are now part of officers', including young officers' and NCOs' education.

Lieutenant General Sir Christopher Wallace, however, drew attention in his after Dinner Speech at this Conference to three factors. 'We are

---

Dr Patrick Mileham was commissioned into the Royal Tank Regiment in 1966. He is currently Reader in Corporate Management and a Governor of the University of Paisley, as well as Visiting Fellow of King's College, Department of Defence Studies, Joint Service Command and Staff College. As Associate Fellow of both Chatham House and RUSI, he has been responsible for setting up this joint series of military ethics conferences and editing proceedings for publication.

dealing with language and at a subject level that is alien to those whom we command' he commented. Soldiers, sailors and airmen need the complex and difficult subject to be put in simple terms. 'They need clarity ... not ambiguity'. Secondly he advised that a commander's 'principal aim is to succeed in his mission, not to pursue morality'. He also added that Michael Ignatieff had written to the effect that maintaining the moral high ground was a 'force enabler, a force multiplier'. 'The 'moral high ground', might be 'the vital ground', indeed the 'centre of gravity'. Consistency in approach and application of force 'can bring symmetry to otherwise asymmetric operations', and defeat 'the charge of double standards'.

On General Wallace's first point, it is worthwhile to emphasize the definition of terms. 'Ethics' comprises the study and articulation of general truths and objective principles; 'morality' is the systematic interpretation and judgement of right and wrong, good and bad; value judgements about subjective human behaviour and relationships are expressed in terms of 'moral' and 'morals'. One should be careful not to treat these words as interchangeable. It is worth adding that all contact between two or more human beings has a moral complexion, particularly if it is supposedly based on trust and expectation, as it is in the everyday activities of truly professional armed forces. Indeed, self-restraint is the beginning of all civilized behaviour, and these same military professionals exist ultimately to promote civil society's freedoms. The recently codified 'Moral Component' in the British Military Doctrine[2] acknowledges a corporate metaphysical ethos, promoting 'military effectiveness' and 'fighting power'. It is expressive of all that is best in the humaneness of military service and actions of the 'civilized soldier'. The 'Physical' means and the objective 'Conceptual' thought-processing activities, the muscle and brains of the armed forces so to speak, are the other components of military effectiveness.

On the subject of language itself, in the months since the Conference, many people around the world have been dismayed by the use and manipulation of figures of speech, analogies and metaphors. President Bush's gaffe in using the word 'crusade' caused enormous damage. 'Decapitation' of the regime's leaders had an unfortunate resonance. The 'smoking gun' was likewise unhelpful as shorthand for weapons of mass destruction: it was too close a metaphor and so trivialized the *casus belli*. Used sparingly, 'shock and awe' was fine for the US home population's perception of what their servicemen were doing early in the invasion, but it became itself too much like the rhetoric of terror, for subsequent stabilization and rebuilding. Real, ghastly memories linger of the experience at the receiving end of the destructive power. Latterly the expression 'sexing up' of 'dodgy' intelligence dossiers has trivialized the most important question of all – the justification for war. Such linguistic devices take on a life of their own, are difficult to render sensibly and faithfully into other languages. Frequently they confuse rather than clarify matters of great moral concern.

Iraq: the Questions

There was of course much political soul-searching in early 2003 during the 'phoney war', after Security Council Resolution 1441 (coercing Iraq to grant weapons inspectors unlimited access) in the autumn of 2002, and before any military intervention in that country. A million people came out on the streets of London to demonstrate against war. We may or may not agree that, if significant undeclared stocks of weapons of mass destruction (WMD) did really exist, then Saddam Hussein morally, legally and defiantly took upon himself the decision-making responsibility of 'last resort', with consequences to himself and his people. It can be concluded that he knowingly and actively provoked a 'just war'. Hunting for the WMD, however, continues to date (April 2004). Lack of evidence continues to cause damage to the British Government's credibility, particularly when connected to the Hutton Inquiry (on the suicide of the scientist Dr David Kelly) and the Butler Inquiry (the role of intelligence) over the *interpretation* of evidence of WMD.

In the event, moral justification for the use of force to coerce Saddam Hussein to destroy such weapons and adhere to SCRs in full, and/or impose regime change in Iraq, relied substantially on the declared military 'successes' of Kosovo and Afghanistan and the rebuilding of those countries. The lack of consensus in the UN and amongst NATO members was based chiefly on doubts about the 'just war' criteria being met. 'Expectation of success', being one of these doubts, required the invasion to be successful, which meant low casualties and a swift conclusion. US and British statesmen and military leaders seemed to base moral intuition and subjective political considerations above what others consider was the precise legal position. Those in favour of a military invasion would have drawn comfort from the view by an Anglican Bishop in March 2003:

> Living in a fallen and broken world, you cannot from time to time escape the reality that taking life may actually be required of us if we are to stop yet worse chaos.[3]

Wisdom for taking military action – or opting for inaction – will be judged by future generations, as well as academics, commentators and *vox populi* in the months and years ahead. The recent capture and detention and future trial of Saddam Hussein brings further questions about the supremacy of law over morality or vice versa.

It must be added that one's thoughts of even a few months ago fade quickly, as do memories of events. Viewed in the days of intense pressure on Iraq *before* hostilities began on 19 March 2003, the outcome seemed to indicate one or a mixture of the following eventualities – an invasion which would work; one that would fail; a protracted war with mixed outcomes; compellance or coercion on the grand scale but short of war, leading to successful disarmament or regime change; a continuing dangerous state of appeasement with worse to come; a popular uprising; an aging Hussein relinquishing power over time; or longer-term democratic processes at work in Iraq for eventually transferring power from dictatorship to parliamentary democracy. These were first-order outcomes. Second- and third-order consequences could have been, or yet may be, a change in the scale and nature of global terrorist activities, collapse of other states, and/or the positive extension of democracy, as well as changes in the dynamics of alliances and domestic politics in Europe and America.

Apparent before, and coming to mind during the conflict, a number of *politico-military-moral* questions emerged. First-order moral problems were:

- the precise interpretation of Rules of Engagement against military targets,
- identifying combatants/non-combatants,
- engaging non-military but 'security' related targets,
- reacting to unclear, fleeting opportunity targets,
- the problem of collateral damage,
- disproportionate overkill and damage,
- the asymmetry of casualties sustained or inflicted,
- claims of immediate humanitarian catastrophe outweighing military advantage.

Second-order moral questions were:

- dealing with collapsing Iraqi military forces and when they ceased to be 'protected' as combatants,
- rules on wearing or discarding uniforms and insignia,
- dealing with civilians as potential combatants or criminals (e.g. check-point suicide bombers, human shields),

- the moral choice between arrest and firing for effect,
- protection of property and preventing looting,
- discipline and the 'moral' right of conscripts of the Iraqi Army to surrender, when faced with overwhelming force and simultaneously being subject to coercion by the Republican Guard,
- the act of 'tipping' military advantage at the operational level.

Even making the distinction between the two categories is open to question. Many of the American, British and other combatant nations were aware of and will continue to reflect on the stark moral contradictions they faced, expressed with clarity by the priest Father Philip Berrigan (who fought as a young man in the Second World War), 'I killed in order to prove the immorality of killing. I massacred in order to demonstrate the illegality of mass murder. I laid waste in order to show that laying waste is unjust'.[4]

Third-order moral questions predominate the present and will remain for months or years to come, such as:

- stabilization and military responsibilities in regard to essential services,
- law and order enforcement and routine policing,
- policing under conditions of mass civil unrest, instantaneous or prolonged,
- the consequences of judicial action against the former President of Iraq,
- the eventual constitutional settlement and political life or Iraq.

Further consequences will undoubtedly reverberate within the political life of the nations involved, between nations who disagreed on the wisdom and practicalities of invasion and future developments within the United Nations itself.

New Chapter

Having therefore concentrated in this third conference in the series, on the moral arguments that reinforce or confound *jus ad bellum*, attention to *jus in bello*, based on the Afghanistan and Iraq experience, inevitably forms the 'new chapter' in the continuing British debate on military ethics. We find there are a number of themes that still need addressing, as well as doctrine and education. Two, in my view, predominate.

The first is the physical risk factor to service personnel in operations. 'Risk', according to Peter L. Bernstein, is active and the word 'derives from the early Italian *risicare*, which means 'to dare'. In this sense, risk 'is a choice rather than a fate.'[5] Danger implies a set of passive circumstances, events or relationships. Mary Warnock asserts that 'moral choices must be free'[6], linking morality with freedom of choice. This reinforces the statement made on two occasions in this conference on the subject of personal responsibility, for both leaders and followers. One is reminded of the existential experience, or 'situational awareness', of the individual soldier, looking through a gun sight, living through Tolstoy's 'moment of moral hesitation which decides the fate of battles'.[7]

In the first Conference in 1998 ('Ethical Dilemmas of Military Operations'), Alastair Duncan (who commanded the First Battalion Prince of Wales's Own Regiment) drew attention to the difficulties of making moral choices and

> Consulting the Law of Armed Conflict in the turret of a Warrior [personnel carrier] at 40 miles an hour, while replying to a potentially very dangerous situation, [which] is not the best way to formulate, take and confirm major policy decisions, especially when there were 'fine points' of international law at issue, and a press crew hard in pursuit.[8]

Enforcing a legal mandate is a duty. Morality is the extent to which all the objective and subjective considerations interrelate in the circumstances, events and relationships of a military operation. These are *practical* considerations of psycho-philosophy, which comprise the self-discipline of taking risks and simultaneously involve discriminating between good and bad behaviour and judging what are right and wrong decisions.

The difficulties lie somewhere near the heart of what constitutes military professionalism. The British Army's doctrine states that 'All British soldiers share the legal right and duty to fight and if necessary, kill, according to their orders, and an unlimited liability to give their lives in doing so'.[9]

This is a paradox: it implies both choice and determinism. Acceptance of paradox and contradiction is one defining characteristic of modern professionalism, even if the military leaders' task remains to clarify complex problems. Some national armies are indeed highly professional: others, unfortunately, even amongst Western liberal democracies, fall very far short of their members, and their supporting populations, accepting 'unlimited liability' and high levels of risk. The comparative natures and quality of armies can be professionally and morally asymmetric, even if in Alliances or Coalitions theoretically they are not. Opting for 'role specialization' in only providing service support arms can be construed as avoiding a national moral responsibility for engaging in combat, when 'actual killing' is the last resort.

The second theme is to do with moral agency: the personal choice and responsibility, whether of the commanders or individual member of the armed forces. In the second Conference conducted by Chatham House in 1999 ('Military Ethics for the Expeditionary Era'), much emphasis was placed on the 'strategic corporal'. 'He', Michael Ignatieff stated, 'is not just strategic in the military sense, crucially he is strategic in the ethical sense'.[10] His actions, his decisions can directly affect the moral success of the military mission or cause its failure. Ascribing responsibility, the philosopher Alasdair MacIntyre asserts that,

> First moral agents so conceived are justifiably and uncontroversially held responsible for that in their actions which is intentional. Secondly they may be justifiably held responsible for incidental aspects of those actions of which they should have been aware. And thirdly they may be justifiably held responsible for at least some of the reasonably predictable effects of their actions.[11]

The words are chosen with great skill, and need careful reading. The imprecision of some words – 'may be', 'aware', 'should' and 'predictable' – is significant. They indicate value judgement. I have already mentioned above three 'orders' of responsibility. The law is helpful when it instructs first-order responsibility, according to the specific rules of engagements, in the military context. The second- and third-order 'may be' responsibilities are to do with *moral* decisions, based on interpretations of non-linear consequences. Third-order consequences arguably require considerable omniscience, yet in the event may be little more than guesswork. The third-order consequences of war against Saddam Hussein's regime will determine the 'just war' judgement of history. The numerous actions at operational and tactical levels will determine the circumstances and relationships in the immediate stabilization and long-term future of Iraq. How to protect agents, whether statesmen, commanders and service personnel – consciously believing they are acting 'reasonably' and in 'good faith' – from causing accidents and unintended consequences, requires close study of real experiences of relatively successful, as well as failed actions, together with complex, comprehensive, real and imaginatively simulated case study scenarios.

How one educates or trains for moral judgement those civilians with world-wide responsibility, as well as those in uniform facing personal danger, and with different degrees of choice, is for future debate. How one simplifies the most complex of existing circumstances, the relationships of protagonists and antagonists, as well as correctly interpreting the past and predicting future events, is a matter of brainpower, language and moral leadership. The best way to develop mental activity, language, and moral leadership is through continuous debate.

'It is a fact', suggests Montaigne, 'that learning... can only teach us *about* wisdom, integrity and resolution'[12]. Our political leaders and uniformed men and women have to live in the real world and *act* with wisdom, integrity and resolution. We are reminded, particularly in the context of asymmetric operations, that many of the persons whom we are asking our armed forces first to defeat and then assist to reconstruct their lives, see their lives as remaining 'poor, nasty, brutish and short' many years into the future. A number of the conference authors end with the appeal to the future of 'humanity' and 'humankind'. Ethics, morality and morals are what makes us better human beings. The law is often inadequate and cannot easily articulate asymmetries. There will continue to be moral ones for a very long time, if not for the whole future of mankind.

NOTES

[1] General Maxwell D. Taylor, 'A Do-it-Yourself Professional Code for the Military' in Lloyd J. Matthews and Dale E. Brown (Eds), *The Parameters of Military Ethics*, (Washington DC, Pergammon Brasseys, 1986), p. 126.

[2] Ministry of Defence (Army), *Design for Military Operations. The British Military Doctrine*, Army Code 71451, 1989 and 1996.

[3] Rt Revd John Gladwin, Bishop of Guildford, *The Times*, 22 March 2003.

[4] Quoted in *The Week*, 21 December 2002, p. 34. For 'actual killing' see Tolstoy's story *The Raid* (Oxford: Oxford University Press, 1982), p. 1.

[5] Peter L. Bernstein, *Against the Gods. The Remarkable Story of Risk* (New York, John Wiley and Sons, 1996), p. 8.

[6] Mary Warnock, *An Intelligent Person's Guide to Ethics* (London, Duckworth, 1998), p. 94.

[7] Leo Tolstoy, *War and Peace* (Oxford: Oxford University Press, 1968 and 1991), p.196.

[8] Alastair Duncan, 'Mission Command in Practice' in Patrick Mileham and Lee Willett (Eds), *Ethical Dilemmas of Military Operations* (London, Royal Institute of International Affairs, 1999), p. 45.

[9] Ministry of Defence (Army), *Soldiering. The Military Covenant*, Army Doctrine Publication, ADP5, Army Code 71642, 2000, p. 1-1.

[10] Michael Ignatieff, 'Handcuffing the Military? Military judgement, rules of engagement and public scrutiny' in Patrick Mileham and Lee Willett (Eds), *Military Ethics for the Expeditionary Era* (London and Washington DC, Royal Institute of International Affairs and Brookings Institute, 2001), p. 28.

[11] Alasdair MacIntyre, 'Social structures and their threats to moral agency' in *Philosophy*, vol 74 no. 289, 1999, p. 312.

[12] Michel de Montaigne, *Essays*, Volume I, No. 25, various editions. (editor's emphasis).

Index